Routledge Revivals

Light from the East

Light from the East collates letters between Hon. P. Arunáchalam of the legislative council of Ceylon and Edward Carpenter, which expand on issues of the Gñanam or divine knowledge. Carpenter edited these letters for publication in 1927 as well as writing additional articles on issues such as desire, birth control and bisexuality in relation to the customs of Ceylon and religious laws of Hinduism to give the reader a broad insight into the religion. This title will be of interest to students of sociology, anthropology and religious studies.

Light from the East

Being Letters on Gñaman, The Divine Knowledge

Hon. P. Arunáchalam
Edited by
Edward Carpenter

First published in 1927
by George Allen & Unwin Ltd

This edition first published in 2016 by Routledge
2 Park Square, Milton Park, Abingdon, Oxon, OX14 4RN
and by Routledge
711 Third Avenue, New York, NY 10017

Routledge is an imprint of the Taylor & Francis Group, an informa business

© 1927 Edward Carpenter

All rights reserved. No part of this book may be reprinted or reproduced or utilised in any form or by any electronic, mechanical, or other means, now known or hereafter invented, including photocopying and recording, or in any information storage or retrieval system, without permission in writing from the publishers.

Publisher's Note
The publisher has gone to great lengths to ensure the quality of this reprint but points out that some imperfections in the original copies may be apparent.

Disclaimer
The publisher has made every effort to trace copyright holders and welcomes correspondence from those they have been unable to contact.

A Library of Congress record exists under LC control number: 70203839

ISBN 13: 978-1-138-18457-2 (hbk)
ISBN 13: 978-1-315-64502-5 (ebk)
ISBN 13: 978-1-138-18461-9 (pbk)

The Hon. P. Arunáchalam
M.A. Cambridge and member of the Legislative Council of Ceylon

Emery Walker ph. sc.

LIGHT FROM THE EAST

BEING LETTERS ON GÑANAM, THE
DIVINE KNOWLEDGE

BY THE
HON. P. ARUNÁCHALAM

EDITED BY
EDWARD CARPENTER

LONDON: GEORGE ALLEN & UNWIN LTD.
RUSKIN HOUSE, 40 MUSEUM STREET, W.C.1

First published in 1927
(All rights reserved)

*Printed in Great Britain by
Unwin Brothers, Ltd., Woking*

CONTENTS

	PAGE
INTRODUCTION	9
EXTRACTS FROM THE LETTERS OF P. ARUNÁCHALAM, SECTION I	31
EXTRACTS DITTO, SECTION II	57
THE LINGAM AND SENSUAL DESIRE	87
THE ENDEAVOUR TO CONTROL DESIRE	109
BIRTH CONTROL AND BISEXUALITY	126
THE MOUNA SWAMIS AND THE ANIMALS	143

INTRODUCTION

THE present period is one in which a liberation of new forces in every department of human activity seems to be pending, and one accordingly which is likely to be rich in events and dramatic *dénouements*; so that almost any contribution to an understanding of the period may prove important. The subject of *Gñanam* (the divine knowledge as it is termed in India and Ceylon), which is dealt with in the present volume, demands attention for the following reason, among others, that for thousands of years the keenest intellects of the East (and no one can deny their general subtlety and penetration) have been occupied with the consideration and hoped-for solution of the great problems of the world and human life—the why and the

Light from the East

wherefore, the whence and the whither of the same—subjects which indeed the more practical Western mind is inclined as a rule to pass by with little or no consideration. And Gñanam may, I take it, be said to be the residual and definite summary by the Indian mind of its conclusions on these far-reaching and difficult topics.

That Gñanam is always right I do not for a moment maintain, but I think it is only reasonable that we of the West should give its conclusions due hearing and consideration.

Too often our attitude towards these great problems has been like that described in Edward FitzGerald's translation of Omar Khayyám:

> "Myself when young did eagerly frequent
> Doctor and Saint, and heard great Argument
> About it and about; but evermore
> *Came out by the same door as in I went*"—

an attitude of familiarity without real intention to reach the heart of the matter.

But if we are to move forward at all it

Introduction

is clear that we must attack these great questions in a different spirit from that. We do not intend to come out always by the same door wherein we went!

There have been two great movements of the human mind (and more no doubt) which will leave their mark on ensuing ages; and these are (1) the effort of the mind (well represented perhaps by the Indian *Upanishads*) to explore its own depths and the process of its own thoughts and speculations; and (2) its effort to understand and analyse the processes and changes of the external world and outer Nature. The importance of the last-mentioned movement is appreciated by everyone under the name of *Physical Science*; the importance of the first-mentioned is now widely recognised under the name of *Psychology*.

In modern Physical Science we see the mind turned outwards and intent on analysing and explaining external Nature in its minutest and most recondite manifestations; in works on the other hand like the Upanishads (or, say, like Wundt's ponderous *Psychology*) we see the same mind turned inwards and intent on tracking down and tabulating the delicate manifestations and expressions of human *feeling*. Both in fact are really occupied in the same quest—the endeavour to locate or define the being who lies at the root of all these experiences, the *ego* itself.

I need hardly say that this last endeavour is utterly and of necessity vain and useless. The *ego* never can and never *will* be caught in the careful net of Science; though doubtless in the long process of pursuit (as in other and similar cases) much that is valuable will be gained.

The coming into touch with the Hon. P. Arunáchalam of the Legislative Council, Ceylon (as shown in this book), gave me an insight into the swift and delicate discriminations of the Eastern mind, while the daily talk which I had with his *guru* (the often

Introduction

quoted "master" or "gñani") during a period of nearly two months, enabled me to gauge pretty thoroughly the meaning of Gñanam—i.e. the philosophy of the Gñanis, who may indeed be counted as the followers in modern times of the great tradition of the Upanishads. Whether these Gñanis have arrived at anything like a permanent and substantial addition to human thought and philosophy is of course a matter on which my readers will hold different opinions.

My own view, and it is a view shared by many of these same thinkers, is that the highest wisdom really consists at present in the ability to *dismiss Thought* and to retain the mind in that state where it perceives events indeed, and is sensitive to them, but does not occupy itself at all with the question of their Why or Wherefore. Of course I recognise that this attitude of mind, if it became general, would be utterly destructive of all the generalisations of Modern Science —whose whole object and *raison d'être* is

Light from the East

the discovery of the so-called Causes of things. But as I began my *academic* career by insisting (in 1890, I think) on the futility of Modern Science, for which ineptitude I was soundly berated by the learned men and professors of that day (or at any rate by those few who deigned to pay attention to my heresies), I shall quite naturally not be heart-broken if I find after all I am right and that the learned ones have in the end come round to my point of view.

In putting, therefore, into print large portions of my friend's letters to me—and that with the cordial approval of his much-honoured widow—a few words of introduction and explanation may not be amiss. Arunáchalam and I had talked over the subject of Gñanam many times—even as far back as Cambridge days—and when, years afterwards, i.e. about the year 1890, Arunáchalam wrote entreating me to *come out* to Ceylon and meet a certain Gñani, who was at that time staying near Colombo,

Introduction

I readily consented. I had, indeed, dreamed of such a *rencontre* and had felt a persuasion that the dream was destined to be fulfilled. It thus happened that I remained in Ceylon —and chiefly in the vicinity of Kurunégala —for two months, and during that time, in company with Arunáchalam, who acted as interpreter, had interviews almost daily with the said Teacher. At a later time, and after I had returned home, Arunáchalam wrote to me pretty frequently. But when, after his death, his widow and the family begged me to write some account of his life and of the Gñani teachings generally, I had to explain that though with my other work this would be impossible I still would gladly make long extracts from his already received letters, which extracts I would send out, and they would serve to answer some of the queries.

The following passages, therefore—it should be explained—are extracts from Arunáchalam's letters—extracts made with a view to their possible circulation some day

Light from the East

in England, and with a view also to the possibility of their being useful to the Arunáchalam family and their friends in Ceylon. It will readily be understood that while I do not agree with everything that is said in the letters I am glad to seize the opportunity of recording how very much I owe not only to Arunáchalam himself for having insisted on my visiting Ceylon, but also to the said Gñani for putting so much of his time at my disposal and for having been willing to answer the hundred and one questions, or smooth out the many difficulties which occurred to me in this connection.

That I have been quite successful in my endeavour to render the nature of Gñanam clear to the Western mind is a thing I can hardly expect; still at the present time, when there is taking place such a decided *rapprochement* between Oriental and Western mentality, I cannot but feel that it is worth while to do what little one can towards bringing the two bodies of thought into

Introduction

touch with each other. In a brief paper, entitled *A Visit to a Gñani*,[1] I have already given some account of my interviews with the Seer in question, and my estimate of his teaching; and to this the reader may be referred; but the actual letters of Arunáchalam to myself, or the portions reprinted here, may clear up points which might otherwise be missed, and may throw light collaterally on many little-known customs of the Wise men and devotees of Gñanam[2] in the East.

The letters are written in a spirit of enthusiasm which I naturally ascribe to the fact that in them my friend was anxious to show in the most favourable light the views of the Gñani whom he represented, as well as the general tenets of Gñanam; but though I do not in every respect share the ardour of my friend's enthusiasm, I am bound to say that I do consider the teaching to be full of important points,

[1] Reprinted by Allen & Unwin in 1920, price 3s. 6d.
[2] Gñanam, of course, *means* Knowledge.

Light from the East

which it would be well for the Western world most seriously to consider. Though I am willing to admit the superiority of the Saivite teaching to our ordinary Western Theology (which is not saying much perhaps!), there are many points on which I disagree with *both*!

What I do much admire in Gñanam (though this may seem surprising to some) is its positive, almost scientific character. I mean that it tries to describe inner facts and matters of actual experience *which can be tested*, and that in consequence its conclusions do not rest for their authority on the mere pronouncements of sacred books or sacred persons but on actual *experience*. For instance, it is generally admitted that one of the first conditions of attainment is the power of the Inhibition of Thought. This power of Inhibition is, of course, difficult, *very* difficult to obtain; but it is obvious that until one attains it one is not qualified to judge of its value and results. All one can say is that those who do really attain

Introduction

become immediately aware that they have reached a turning-point in the great process of evolution. The change of direction is self-evident. The third stage of human evolution has been approached, and a new vista towards the future opens out before one.

I may here quote some passages from my own book, *Pagan and Christian Creeds*,[1] where we find (p. 250) these words :—

"The second stage of human psychologic evolution is an aberration, a divorce, a parenthesis. With its culmination and dismissal the mind passes back into the simple state of union with the Whole. (This is the state of Ekagráta in the Hindu philosophy : one-pointedness, singleness of mind.) And the consciousness of the Whole, and of things to come and of things far around—which consciousness had been shut out by the concentration on the local self—begins to return again. This is not to say, of course, that the *excursus* in the second stage has been a loss and a defect. On the contrary, it means that the Return is a bringing back of all that has been gained during the period of exile (including all sorts of mental and technical knowledge and skill, emotional developments, instincts, finesse and adaptability of mind),

[1] Allen & Unwin.

Light from the East

a bringing of these things *back* into the harmony with the Whole. It means, ultimately, a great gain. The Man, perfected, comes back to a vastly extended harmony. He enters again into a real understanding and confidential relationship with his physical body, and with the body of the society in which he dwells—from both of which he had been sadly divorced ; and he takes up again the broken thread of the Cosmic Life."

All this is a matter of positive experience, and that is why I say that Gñanam has (so far) a scientific character.

The Inhibition of Thought is certainly difficult, but it is *necessary* ; it is indeed the beginning of that Divine Knowledge whose end is liberation from Mortality. It is the vestibule and door of approach to an altogether larger world of which we are now in these latter days only slowly becoming aware. It is the door of approach to one of the central doctrines of Gñanam—the realisation of the Motionless Intelligence, or Gñana-akása. That kind of Intelligence (it will be seen at once) is in the clearest and most undeniable contrast to our ordinary and worldly intelligence. The latter is

Introduction

in constant and unceasing *Motion*. That is almost its supreme boast. It being our present Ideal to be constantly darting " swift as Thought " hither and thither, the very notion of a mentality *ceasing to move* conveys an effect almost of *paralysis*. But Gñana-akása is (as the very juxtaposition of the two words would seem to imply) the very reverse of paralysis. It is the knowledge which *is* Space. It is the identification of Space with Consciousness. It is the medium *within* which Thought may indeed move, but which far surpasses all Thought and imagination in the width and swiftness of its embrace.

I may here quote from Arunáchalam himself (see the *Letters*) :

"The space that fills all pots and houses is one. It is differentiated by thought according to the varieties of outer covering, as Brahmin, Outcast, King, Beggar, Palace, Hut. But there is no differentiation in space. So in the pure unagitated Intelligence there is no differentiation. Therefore was it graciously said (by Tiruvalluvar) in the Tirukkural (6th verse of the chapter on

Light from the East

Renunciation), 'He who has destroyed the conceit of "I" and "mine" will enter a world higher than that of the celestials.' And Tayumanavar says, 'When, oh! when shall I realise the truth of the teaching that to know the knower is the true wealth?'"

To know the knower! Is this possible? The very idea implies the folding back of the mind on itself, and suggests the possibility—even the probability—of the mind becoming at times unduly strained in the process.

I think, indeed, that this last is a danger to be guarded against. No one can read the accounts of these candidates for "illumination"—whether in the East or in the very modern West—of their queer ways, their frequent lapsing into vain repetitions or glaring imbecility, without seeing that on this path there are pitfalls. We do not want, and we do not *intend* to become imbeciles on our way to heaven! and though it may be perfectly true that the phrase "to know the knower" represents in brief compass an extraordinary attainment, it does

Introduction

not follow that that attainment is open or advisable for everybody.

There is a certain contradiction of terms in all this. There is no instruction or rule in Gñanam more definite than the following: that one must not allow the mind to wander *out of itself* in the search for any external good. The mind by its very nature and holy origin *contains everything in itself*; to lean outwards, therefore, on something external is to be false to one's true self; the very effort of *seeking* salvation destroys that which one seeks. The only true way is *not* to seek. And so the Gñanis say that:

> "As a bird returning to its nest folds its wings at the last moment and is carried on by its already acquired speed, so the loving soul arrives at the last where it would be—and *that* without hesitation or strain."

To make an effort would obviously destroy the bird's chance of success, for the folding of the wings is indispensable—as indeed every true lover knows with regard to his

Light from the East

heart's desire. He must move with a kind of superhuman faith, and a certain knowledge that his need is in the great line of his destiny.

In the holy places of the Saivite temples there is generally a figure of the God Siva in the attitude of a Dancer—" The Dancing God" he is called (O thou that dancest the dance of endless joy in the spacious halls of Pure Consciousness!). What a lovely conception of a God! Yet sometimes, no doubt, it has been thought unworthy of a great religion thus to show its central figure occupied in what the West would probably call a frivolous waste of time. (Imagine, for instance, the Christian devotees worshipping a dancing Jesus!) But such criticisms only expose the petty mental outlook of those who make them. No figure, surely, could symbolise the Freedom and Joy of the Creator and his endless resource more *perfectly* than the figure of a Dancer—throwing out forms of grace without ceasing and creating

Beatrice Bundy photographer   Emery Walker ph sc.

Edward Carpenter
from a photograph taken 12th November 1912

Introduction

beauty by merely liberating his own energies. Here again we have Gñana-akása, knowledge without place, the motionless Intelligence. For in that world—of the Soul—there are really no dark places. When you are ready for the next move, illumination comes to you, and comes often in the most unexpected shape and place. (See the *Letters*, or see *T.D.*,[1] p. 233.)

"The Mother shall wear herself out with domestic duties and attending to her children; she shall have no time to herself, yet before she dies, her face shall shine like heaven:
The Magdalen shall run down to answer the knock at the door, and Jesus, her lover, himself shall enter in."

"You met my brother" (the letter continues) "some years ago in England, and if you saw him now you would be able to judge of the change—so calm and happy and wise, of a truthfulness and courage that nothing can shake, fearing nothing, desiring

[1] *Towards Democracy.*

Light from the East

nothing, so sympathetic and loving—and with such a charm of manner and face, the reflection of the calm and peace within."

It is, indeed, a blaze of consciousness which is indicated by that phrase " to know the knower "—so it may well be that it is wise not to pry into it too closely ! lest indeed one should be consumed in the blaze. (See Chapter II in my little book, *A Visit to a Gñani*, also especially pp. 7, 8 and 9 in the same book.)

In all this there is much, as I have said before, that reminds one of the manifestations of Sex in the Body ; the fixed, almost rigid state into which the body falls on the very edge of its creative effort, the threads like lightning streaming from all parts of the organism to their fulfilment ; the ecstatic deliverance, the man becoming God, and so forth. The unalloyed pure consciousness is there, burning and blazing in the depths ; and the world which we know—the world of actual life and experience—is derived from that one by a process which we

Introduction

can best perhaps describe as a process of alloy, of watering down, of dilution. It being (in modern life) our ideal to be constantly darting swift as Thought, hither and thither, the very notion of mentally ceasing to move is to most moderns repugnant and depressing. But " the pure intelligence (Arivu) is impartite spirit-space (Gñana-akása), nothing else. It becomes fettered by the thought which differentiates the body and its faculties, its experiences and spheres, as ' I ' and ' mine '; and is emancipated if that differentiation ceases "—i.e. when the motionless intelligence is realised as God.

I may, in concluding this introductory chapter, dwell for a moment on some characteristics of Arunáchalam himself. One of these was (to me at least, since my own mind works rather slowly) the surprising *rapidity* of his thought. And with this rapidity went, as its natural accompaniment, an extreme *receptivity*. I was often impressed by the ease and celerity with which he drank in and absorbed all sorts of difficult and recondite matters (doubly difficult to a foreigner) as, e.g., a question of procedure in the House of Commons, while at the same time this receptiveness was healthily counterbalanced by a certain almost elfish spirit of chaff and opposition which one might notice at times.

This last peculiarity is, I am inclined to think, characteristic of the Tamils, who are noted for their originality and their sturdy independence of mind. For the Tamils, indeed as a people, I have always felt a strange sympathy and admiration. Their perception of the Occult and the Magical is quite remarkable and is felt, I believe, as a pervasive influence in their philosophy and Poetry. I have sometimes heard Anglo-Indians (trying perhaps to justify the widely accepted dogma of British superiority) call the Tamils " niggers " or " dusky demons," or by some name even less complimentary —but in most of these cases I have felt that the *sobriquet* was really an unconscious tribute

Introduction

to the powers and insight of this remarkable people who, in many respects, are quite beyond the understanding of the ordinary Britisher.

EXTRACTS FROM
THE LETTERS OF P. ARUNÁCHALAM

SECTION I

ALEXANDRA HOUSE,
CINNAMON GARDENS,
COLOMBO, CEYLON.
Nov. 25th, 1888.

MY DEAR FRIEND,
. . . O that you were here to meet and commune with the only man I have known who is a seer and not one blindly groping in the dark. He has given me the priceless blessing of belief in God, which my English education had robbed me of for the last twenty years, and he has enabled me to enter the threshold of the mysteries of our religion, which in my folly begotten of arrogance and the material West, in my impatience of forms and ceremonies that I did not understand, I made

Light from the East

light of. I never knew till now what sacred truths underlie these forms, and that the latter are but a preparation for those higher stages on the first rung of which I am now placed by God's grace and the Guru (teacher) he has sent me. How ignorant and blind other religions, and irreligion, are! How all the latest discoveries of European so-called science, all creeds, systems of thought are but sparks from the Truth here enshrined! How they all merge in this ocean!

* * * * *

I believe it is possible for man, if ripe enough, to see God and to be one with him while yet imprisoned in the body. Many men have done so, and I know one at least who, under our Guru's teaching, is very near.

* * * * *

I want you, my friend, to know the Way. Your life seems to have been a preparation for the high stages for which the *ordinary* run of mankind must qualify by the obser-

Letters of P. Arunáchalam

vances of the rites, forms, injunctions of the exoteric religion of the Hindus. You of all my friends are most ripe. So come out to the East and seek the truth. This has been discovered in India because our greatest men have through thousands of years devoted themselves to its pursuit.

* * * * *

But these matters I ought not, in my ignorance, to have ventured to write about. They should be explained to you by your Guru. I only throw out hints—blind and misleading, I fear—in my anxiety that you, my dearest friend, may see something of what has been working within me and may be moved to seek and win in this life what I shall perhaps not get for long, long ages.

* * * * *

TANJORE, INDIA.
December 27th, 1889

MY DEAR CARPENTER,

... I have been here about six weeks. Tanjore is a great centre of Tamil civilisation and was till about thirty years ago the capital of a native dynasty. The last line of kings was Mahrattas and succeeded the ancient Tamil dynasty of the Cholas after a brief rule of the Nayaks. Unjustly deprived of their throne by the English, the representatives of the last dynasty are now here in various stages of poverty and distress. Here also, but in far greater and pitiable destitution, are the descendants of the last native dynasty of *Ceylon*. A good deal of the time of the royal folks is spent in building castles in the air and scheming for increased allowances and restoration of the throne.

I have come here to be alone with the Master of whom I wrote to you in my last and who first raised for me a corner of the veil that hides the mysteries of the universe. I shall have to return to Ceylon in about a fortnight to my work, but it is daily becoming more and more irksome and I must rid myself of the bondage, for a time at least, that I may go my way at leisure and

Letters of P. Arunáchalam

undistracted. I hope to return to Tanjore sometime next year and live near the Master for about a year.

* * * * *

The term *Saivam* is a derivative form of *Sivam* (the Auspicious, i.e. God) and is the equivalent of *Siva Sambandam*, i.e. that which is bound (band), with (sam), God (Sivam). Wherever God is, there is Saivam. As there is nothing in which God is not, nothing is alien to Saivam. No religion, philosophy, belief, caste or race but is part of Saivam. Each reveals so much of the truth and in such shape as suits the degree of ripeness of the souls to be benefited thereby, and so by degrees enlightened and purified they become fit to receive the whole truth.

That universal, pure, absolute consciousness, which we call God, shines everywhere brilliantly or dimly, according to the purity or otherwise of the case in which it happens to be enclosed. It is like space, all pervading and equal, alike in hut and palace, in outcast and Brahmin, in Vishnu, Brahma, Christ, Buddha, you, me, the meanest worm or stone. Unlike the material space the God-space is eternal (sat), intelligent (chit), blissful (ananda)—or to translate the words more correctly it is, pure being, pure consciousness, pure bliss, bearing in mind that there is in it no difference between subject and object. Except for its illumination we are powerless to see, feel, hear, think, even as the eye cannot see save with the help of light of sun or moon or lamp of some sort. It permeates and vitalises all things and gives life and light to all, from a tuft of grass to the highest deity.

* * * * *

Shortly before I left Tanjore, I went to Chidambaram (near Pondicherry), the seat of a celebrated temple whose age must be counted by thousands of years, a magnificent structure like most temples in southern India. It is the typical temple of Saivam and shows side by side its exoteric and esoteric aspects. Here is clearly shown the curriculum which Saivam has graciously provided, adapted to the spiritual and intellectual needs of all, and whereby they may with ease graduate in the knowledge of the One Reality. Services and prayers are the only course recognised by Christianity (besides, doubtless, good conduct, as in other religions). Yet she fails equally to reach the lower strata of humanity and the most cultured classes, being suited only to the tastes of the staid and dull middle classes. Temple services and prayers are prescribed only in the lower classes of the Saivite curriculum. Yet they are so well designed as to attract the dullest brute no less than the most sensitive temperament and the most cultured intellect; elaborate ritual, lights, music, dances, in the daily services; countless festivals; pilgrimages to sacred shrines and streams: these, while gratifying the religious emotions of the people, provide for them all through the year and gratis, theatres and opera houses in every town and village, and

Light from the East

open-air entertainments on hill and stream. Gradually purified in spirit, they are led up to the higher stages in which there is neither ritual, prayer, nor worship of any sort known to the other religions of the world, nor any distinction of caste or race.

* * * * *

As I write, I overlook a lovely lake, one of the grand artificial lakes made by the Native Kings centuries ago to irrigate the rice fields of this once populous, rich district. But now the population has dwindled till you can hardly get men to work in the fields; and the tank, recently restored, remains nearly useless. The disease-stricken, miserable people I frequently come across in this province make me miserable. Some time ago I should have considered suicide the only relief to them and to us who cannot relieve their distress. But I know now that that is no relief, deeds and their consequences cannot be so easily strangled. But there is no ground for despair. Things hard to bear or to relieve must be borne bravely as the just retribution of past acts, and then the soul in its evolution will find in this or in another life a happier sphere for its development. Life is a poor miserable affair unless it is regarded as a training-ground for the soul, a place where it may by worthily discharging its duties, and experiencing its sorrows and joys, purify itself and gain a knowledge of, and become its true self, i.e. God. I used to think some months ago, the entanglements of my life an insuperable obstacle and that I must run away and be alone. I feel now that that is a mistake and that amid any surroundings one may progress if one is true to oneself. What a comfort it has been to realise, however dimly, that in the least things as in the greatest, we are led on for our own good, as though with hidden strings, by an ever-watching Providence—led on, stumbling, falling, rising, marching, falling again—while all the time we delude ourselves with the thought that it is all our doing!

Light from the East

Well, in the Chidambaram temple, of which I was speaking when I broke off, there is, as in other Hindu temples, elaborate ritual, distinction (but not so marked) of caste and race, etc. In the innermost shrine is the image of Siva in the attitude of a dancer—the Dancing God he is called here, the dance symbolising the operations of the universe. Immediately behind the sacred image hangs a curtain which screens off the Holy of Holies, the Great Mystery as it is called. It is a privilege rarely accorded to look behind the curtain. But the mercenary priests can be induced to make exceptions. I was granted the privilege some years ago after a good deal of fuss, and again on this visit. What do you think I saw behind the curtain? Emptiness—mere space. I did not understand it on my first visit nor do the priests. The thing is clear to me now as explained by the Master, and so I find it is explained in the books. The essence of Saivam, as I have said, is Equality. This is typified by the space behind the curtain. (What the curtain typifies you will learn from your Guru). But Equality is not confined, as among the Westerners to human beings (or should I say white men?) but embraces all living things as well as the things called not living because the Divine consciousness in them is not apparent to our coarser senses. Equality underlies the dance in the Universe, as in the temple worship it underlies the ritual.

* * * * *

The social upheavals that threaten the life of nations in Europe cannot occur in India in spite of the ravages of English education. Material comfort and luxury are not here the aim of life. They are far more generally diffused than in Europe, thus giving the poorest the opportunity to cherish and to attain nobler ideals. Thanks to our climate and to our simple customs, how little a man wants in the East and how easily he may acquire it! The energies of Europeans are so exhausted in the struggle

Light from the East

with their surroundings and in providing themselves with the necessaries of life that no wonder they have hardly time to think of anything else. The weak are crushed in the struggle, and the strong, elated by their success, are led away by the Will of the Wisp of luxury to bury themselves deeper and deeper in the mire of Maya, and further and further away from the light.

* * * * *

The people live simply. The highest education and culture, unless it be of the English sort, are compatible with the simplest life. The Master, for instance, who has to support his wife, two grown-up sons and the wife and children of the elder son—all living together, as usual in Indian Families—does it on Rs. 60, equal to less than £4 a month. My expenditure comes to at least £100 a month, though my own share, I am glad to say, is little. I have made a complete revolution in my mode of life. I have been a vegetarian for eighteen months

Letters of P. Arunáchalam

and otherwise simplified my wants in a manner that would have been incredible a couple of years ago. For a man of the Master's stamp to support two families in comfort and dignity would be, I suppose, inconceivable in England. He is certainly far the most cultured and educated man I know. A vigorous, practical intellect which finds no subject too great or too small, which handles thoroughly and masters everything it takes up—whether an abstruse problem of philosophy, an intricate law-suit, or the cooking of some appetising dish—devoting undivided attention to the subject in hand until it is disposed of; unrivalled power of exposition, and a purity and loftiness of character which nothing can shake. What else can a man be who has attained his spiritual height! The freaks of passion which cloud the intellect of the so-called men of genius do not trouble him. There is no Self ever bobbing up like a Jack-in-the-box. The divine light within shines forth pure and serene. What a contrast to

Light from the East

Carlyle with his miserable selfishness, struggles with his stomach and his wife, oaths and curses! Call him a wise man!

*　　*　　*　　*　　*

Our Master is no Ascetic. Like Socrates he enjoys worldly comforts when he has them; when he has them not, he does not miss them. But *his* Master was a vigorous ascetic. He was a wealthy merchant and abandoned home in the prime of life and roamed over forest and mountain, a true child of Nature, as sentimental Europeans would call him, but I would call him Master of Nature, or rather Nature herself, for had he not become one with the God-space I was speaking of? He made no difference in his way of living when he found himself in towns. He would go about unwashed and naked. A king or pariah, man or dog alike to him. He would lie with equal dignity and indifference on a dust-heap or in a palace. The same to him whether he was feasted and worshipped or abused and ill-treated. A magnificent specimen, physically, of the Genus *homo* ; a true king among men. To outward appearance a madman, yet when he chanced to speak in private to his favorite disciple, a flood of wisdom poured forth. It was not the man speaking, but the God within directly and in all purity, unclogged by the coarse environments which imprison us ordinary mortals.

* * * * *

As we are taught, there are three means employed by God in His infinite Grace for illuminating the soul—(1) Revealed Scriptures; (2) the Guru who comes to you when you are ripe and comes often in most unexpected shape and place (cf. Christ's coming to Peter and Andrew, James and John, and to Matthew); (3) Self-experience. The Guru only says what is in the Scriptures, but which has remained veiled till his arrival. Nothing that he or the

Light from the East

Scriptures say must be thought true unless confirmed by your own experience.

* * * * *

You met my brother some years ago in England and if you saw him now you would be able to judge of the change. What a high spiritual and intellectual level he has reached! So calm and happy and wise, and of a truthfulness and courage that nothing can shake.

* * * * *

> KURUNÉGALA, CEYLON.
> *15th February,* 1891.

MY DEAR CARPENTER,

... The Cesarewitch's tour must have revealed to him England's weakness in India. You ought to read Digby's powerful statement in *India* of January 16th. It is quite heart-rending, the terrible destitution of the people all over the country, and he shows it to be the direct result of English rule. How well it confirms the

Letters of P. Arunáchalam

Master's views! Digby's remarks are not less true of Ceylon. Only this week has been published a despatch of the Governor to the Secretary of State reporting the pitiable condition of the peasantry of the Uva province. All this terrible destitution and suffering, throughout one-seventh of the world's population, has been brought about without any benefit to the English people themselves. It has only benefited the English capitalists and professional classes. The vaunted administrative capacity of the English is a fiction. They make good policemen and keep order, when the people acquiesce—that is all. If this acquiescence ceases, as it must, when the people rightly or wrongly believe their religion and family life in danger from the Government, the English must pack up and go, and woe to the English capitalists and professional men! I feel more and more strongly every day that the English with their commercial ideals and standards and institutions have done far more to ruin the

Light from the East

country than if it had been overrun periodically by hordes of savage Tartars. Physically the people are starving, spiritually they are dead—all who have come within the range of this blizzard.

* * * * *

NUWARA ELIA.
18th September.

MY DEAR FRIEND,

... Experiencing whatever happens, free from anxiety, if you (standing as " pure consciousness "), perform without attachment whatever work is before you, then that which you now are distressed to have missed, will come to you of itself. It is pure consciousness which stands as the place for the evolution of the thought-shaped Universe; the involution and cessation of that thought-shaped Universe is *Maunam*.[1] This is *Saiva siddhantam*. The end of *siddhantam* is the bliss of Sivam (Sivánandam). Those who reject as unreal all that is known

[1] Silence or cessation of thought.

(objectively) by the consciousness and ever stand as pure consciousness, will become of the shape of *Sat-chit-anandam* (pure being, pure consciousness, pure bliss, where there is no difference between subject and object).

Therefore when you have no work, accustom yourself to be free from thought and to stand as consciousness. When you study, study as consciousness.

NETHERCOURT, COLOMBO.
17th September, 1893.

MY DEAR FRIEND,

. . . Partly idleness and aversion to letter writing, partly great pressure of official work, and during the last two or three months serious illness at home of my wife and of Mahadeva (the latter rescued almost from the grave and not quite well yet) have prevented me from writing. I have for some time past been most anxious to write and tell you of the great calamity that has overtaken me in the loss of our dear Master. He is of course not really lost

Light from the East

to us but is as present and ready to help as ever. But I cannot yet realise this. The long association in my mind of him with the body in which he appeared to us, has left a void not to be filled—and I keep thinking when again I shall see that gracious face and hear those gracious words, so full of comfort and help and strength. How merciful God has been to me to bring me under the Master's influence! Alas, how unworthy I have been of Him and how far from the goal he ever kept before me and by his presence, encouragement, and advice tried to make me reach!

July 18th—Tuesday morning at 3.30 a.m.—was the memorable day of his attainment, as we say, of *paripuranam*, "fullness"—the fullness of emancipation or *mukti* which till then he had enjoyed in limited measure while in the body (*déka*) but which now he enjoys in fullness freed from the body (*vidéka-mukti*), having entered into never-ending union with the bliss of Sivam (Sivá-nandam)

Letters of P. Arunáchalam

You are aware that last year he suffered severely and for some months from an attack of Kurunégala fever. When I wrote to him last year expressing my great sorrow about his illness which he had contracted for yours and my sakes, he wrote:

"The body is a case full of the worm called diseases. Kurunégala fever is a fictitious name. We must not at all be sorry about it." At the end of December on my visit to him at Tanjore I found him quite recovered and able to go about, exerting himself not a little to make me and my family comfortable, and with *such* hospitality. He was greatly reduced in body but he told me the fever had really not affected his true self, and that during the long and severe illness when his wife and son were most despondent about his recovery, he was, for nearly a month, not conscious of his body but remained pure consciousness.

This year he had been quite well and used to write me once or twice a month. His last communication was an acknowledgment

Light from the East

of a money order I had sent him early in July. His letters were full of the usual help, encouragement and comfort. Towards the end of April he wrote:

"One must clearly realise that the Intelligence which, shaken by the wind desire, regards wife, children, etc., as 'mine'; and the body, senses, intellectual organs, etc., as 'I,' is *Jiva* (the individual Soul); that the unagitated Intelligence which regards the intelligence in all manifested things, in wife and child, in ant and elephant, and in oneself, as the one *Sivam*, is *Sivam*. The space that fills all pots and houses is one. It is differentiated by thought according to the varieties of outer coverings as Brahmin, outcast, King, beggar, palace, hut. But there is no differentiation in space. So in the pure unagitated Intelligence there is no differentiation. Therefore was it graciously said (by Tiruvalluvar) in the Tirukkural (6th verse of the chapter on Renunciation):—

"'He who has destroyed the conceit of

Letters of P. Arunáchalam

" I " and " mine " will enter a world higher than that of the celestials.

" 'So Tayumanavar : "When, oh ! when, shall I realise the truth of the teaching that to know the knower is the true wealth ! " '

" These texts should be carefully considered."

In the latter part of June, in acknowledging a letter in which I conveyed to the Master the purport of your last letter, he wrote, and this may be taken as his last message to you—" While Carpenter endeavours to introduce the practice of suppression of thought among the Westerners, he ought also to teach fully that save to those who have gained the freedom from attachment to things which is called *nir-asai* (absence of desire), the knowledge of the *Meipporul* (Truth, the One Reality) is 'difficult' (which may also mean 'impossible') of attainment."

I often think how wonderful it is that you should have been brought in contact with him. About forty years ago Tillainatha

Light from the East

Swamy told him an Englishman would come to him and he should initiate him. Soon after the initiation he (Tillainatha) disappears, as if he had lingered here only for this purpose. One begins to realise now what a speck forty years is in the history of a soul.

I must tell you something about his last days on earth. He was in his usual good health till Sunday morn the 16th July when he sat down to breakfast, but he rose without eating and went and reclined on his couch. The fever showed itself then and he knew his time had come. On the entreaty of his wife and younger son Soma-sundaram (who has been a very devoted son, a great contrast to his elder brother who is still rather a vagrant), he took some medicine, but told them it would not do the illness any good, that they should not weep for him, as he would still remain with them as he ever did before, and that there were certain reasons (which he did not mention) for his being troubled with physical ailments.

Letters of P. Arunáchalam

(I wonder if the reason was what he had often told me, that the communication of the mysteries of God to unripe souls always brought punishment to the teacher. However, he said it was not in his nature to tell things by halves—he must say all or nothing. To say less savoured of dishonesty. It causes me bitter pangs to think that he came to Kurunégala and contracted the dreadful fever on my and your account.) During this last illness he spoke little but remained absorbed in himself. On Monday night, or rather Tuesday morning at 3.30, the vital breath seemed to stop.

As usual in the case of those who attain *sat-chit-ananda*, the body was bathed and anointed and all ceremonies performed as to Siva himself, and was carried to an underground room built for the occasion in a land adjoining the river and was placed in the attitude of *nishtai* (devotion or perfection) and the entrance was covered with a stone and plastered over. Cremation, usual among Hindus, is prohibited in such a case, as the

Light from the East

vital breath is believed to remain in the body for thousands of years, rendering it exempt from corruption. It is proposed to build a temple of Siva, placing a *lingam* at the spot. Meanwhile daily services, as in a temple, are performed there. This then is the completion of that noble life—the man has become God. It is dreadful to think of the ages of toil and suffering still before us and millions and millions of our fellow-creatures before we reach this goal. Lord help us!

EXTRACTS FROM
THE LETTERS OF P. ARUNÁCHALAM

SECTION II

You will be interested in the following short *account of the Master* furnished to me some time ago in his life-time at my request by his son *Soma-sundaram* and which of course tallies with all the Master has told me.

"Our grandmother, Madame Kavérí (name of the Great South Indian river), had at the beginning only one child, a girl. In its infancy it was attacked with a serious illness. While the child was lying in a hopeless condition, my grandmother lay asleep in great sorrow embracing it. She then saw a dream. God Muruga (the God of War and of Wisdom also called *Subra-*

manya) wearing the ochre garments of an ascetic, his hair dressed like a crown with *uruttraksha* beads (nuts of the Eleocarpus Ganitrus worn by Mendicants), appeared spear in hand. She pointed to the child and said, 'Lord, behold her state.' The God said, 'Foolish woman, call *this* a child? In the sixth month from now there will enter your womb a devotee of mine. *He* will be a child to you.' She woke from her dream and the child was dead. According to the words of the God Muruga, my father was conceived six months afterwards and was born. Even in childhood he was distinguished for love of God which arose naturally in him. From his sixteenth year he devoted himself zealously to the worship of the God Muruga. One day while reading by himself in the Chapel of the God in the Great Temple at Tanjore (the Chapel is that beautiful one of Subramanya, referred to on page 215 of your *Adam's Peak to Elephanta*), sleep came over him. He dreamed that he saw a divine assembly in

Letters of P. Arunáchalam

the middle of which on a throne, surrounded by Rishis and Siddhas, sat the God Muruga in ochre robes and sacred ashes and *uruttraksha* beads and hair worn like a crown. *My father* (i.e. our friend the Gñani) at once went and prostrated himself in worship before the God who, according to what is stated in the Saiva Scriptures, placed his foot on my father's head, stroked it with his hand and rubbed the ashes on it, and wrote letters on his tongue, and graciously saying, 'We will come hereafter to initiate you,' he disappeared. My father, waking, praised the love and mercy of the God. Henceforward there came to him as if by instinct the knowledge of *grammar* [1] and other sciences, the philosophy of the Saiva, Siddhanta and Vedanta, the occult lore of the Siddhas, etc. He began to hunger for the knowledge of the Truth which is the end of all things. While thus hungering, he proceeded on a worldly errand to Kumba-Konam, a city twenty-one miles from Tanjore.

[1] Explanation of the name *Elukhanam*.

Light from the East

According to the promise of the God that he would come by and by as Teacher, Tillaináyaka Swami came before him to feed *him*, i.e. the Gñani, with the food of Grace, like a mother that feeds her hunger-stricken children. It is said in our peerless Saiva Agamas that as soon as the Teacher is *seen* or his voice is *heard* by those souls that are ripe, they are drawn to him as iron to the magnet, and the way forthwith is shown of attaining the Truth that is everywhere. So Tillaináyaka Swami appeared to my father and initiated him. Then practising the suppression of thought, he served Tillaináyaka Swami. When the goal was reached, Tillaináyaka Swami said to my father, 'There is no difference between house and forest. You may remain in domestic life,' and departed from Tanjore. Then my father came and lived in Tanjore."

My brother, Rama-Nathan, is pretty well engrossed in his official work (as Solicitor-General) and his writings. He has resumed his "Jesus." Bonser, of Christ's, Cambs., your contemporary, is coming out here as Chief Justice. You will be sorry to hear Justice Telang[1] of Bombay is dead.

Mahadeva, who is by me, asks me to convey to you his love. Accept also mine.

GALLE, CEYLON.
28th February, 1893.

MY DEAR CARPENTER,

You will be glad to know that the Master does not take the view I stated in my last letter as to the inexpediency of your publishing esoteric teaching. I was then only repeating what he has often told to me and, I think, to you also, at Kurumégala. But he evidently thinks the time has now come for publication. Your book may, he thinks, help some ripe soul in sore need of such hints to reach the goal.

In a previous letter he writes :—

" The pure intelligence (' Arivu ') is impartite spirit-space (Gñana-akása), nothing

---

[1] This Justice Telang was an admirable man (Mahratta) whom I much admired and respected (see *Adam's Peak to Elephanta*, p. 299).—E. C.

Light from the East

else. It becomes fettered by the thought which differentiates this body and its intellectual faculties, its experiences and spheres, as 'I' and 'mine'; and is emancipated if that differentiation ceases. As a means to the attainment of this intelligence which is *chit-akása*, gods and shrines and streams and ritual and teachers, etc., have been made. These, however, for persons of petty understanding only. For those of higher and more powerful intelligence is prescribed the study of the Shastras and of the motionless Intelligence as God."

* * * * *

I have, within the last fortnight, come across two Seers of first rank—one of them a strange weird man, who has spent much time in the forests of Anuradhapura, and with a face of the most child-like simplicity and serenity. Neither of them so great in exposition as the Master. This last man of the forests would have much attraction for you. Both are Tamils.

Letters of P. Arunâchalam

TANJORE.
27th July, 1898.

MY DEAR C.,

... I am here on a few days' leave—the first holiday I have had for five and a half years. I came here to attend the anniversary puja or religious ceremony in commemoration of the Master's departure. The ceremony took place on the 23rd inst.—the usual ceremonies that occur in the temple of Siva on grand occasions, together with feeding of over a thousand persons. On the site where his body is interred is a Lingam to which the worship is offered as to the Master. It is remarkable to note the piety and reverence of the crowd. The Master's widow was also there, a gentle, gracious lady full of love and kindness, still the support and comfort of the whole household, including the vagrant Samanathan's family; the latter still rebellious and fighting and unhappy in his soul, but very interesting and learned—and destined no doubt to win peace in the end, for Tillaináyaka Swami has blessed him. The younger

Light from the East

brother Soma-sundarampillai takes after the Master—very practical and sensible and helpful—and bravely bears the burden of the family and does the daily prayer to the Master. The Samadhi building is a simple brick building thatched with coco-nut leaf, and is situated in an acre of ground, which his (Soma-sundaram) energy has converted into a garden from which flowers and fruits and water are obtained for the worship. It is proposed to make a substantial building and roof it with stone, and when the plans are mature, I shall let you know that you may, if convenient, send your mite.

I am starting to-night for Madura and shall be back at home on the 31st. I think you have seen the temple there. It is the great temple of Sakti (the cosmic energy).

"Hailed by the Lord Siva as the Mother of millions of world clusters, yet Virgin by the Vedas called."

I spent some happy days there last week.

Now I must close. May peace ever rest with thee! I enclose some sacred ashes

Letters of P. Arundchalam

from the Master and from the Mouna Swami of Kumbakonam. As I write, I observe one hurrying along the road, with a little bit of cloth between his thighs—and Somasundarampillai who is by me says he is a Great Swami, who has for some time lived in this town, lying on dust-heaps, etc., speaking to no one, seeking no one, eating anything he can get, and worshipped by the people.

In England he would long since have been clapped in gaol.

* * * * *

In the Master's Samadhi garden is a well, sunk at a cost of Rs. 200, which represents what you sent, with the interest thereon. The well is most useful and has fertilised the soil, which is rather poor.

On Board "The Lady Gordon,"
Off Batticaloa,
E.P., Ceylon.
13th <i>March</i>, 1898.

My dear Friend,

. . . I sent you a message by A. M. Bose who was here some months ago on his way to Cambridge with his sons. I hope

Light from the East

you met him. A beautiful simple character. The world has not affected him. He is, I see, doing very good work in England in exposing the dangerous incompetence of the Indian Government in setting everybody by the ears and gagging the mouths of those who point out the danger. The art of administration is a lost art in India. General Gordon, when he came out as P.S. to Lord Ripon and chucked up the place, expressed himself very strongly about the inefficiency and frivolity of Anglo-Indian officials. His prophecies are being fulfilled. The Indian Govt. by its wanton extravagance in useless frontier wars, its oppressive taxes necessitated by such extravagance and by a too costly administration, by its utter want of sympathy with the people who specially need it in this miserable time of plague and famine, and by its cruel treatment of patriots like Tilak who are the only well-wishers of the British rule (for they alone can appreciate its benefits and the dangers if it ceased to be), also by the suppression of reasonable

Letters of P. Arunâchalam

and fair comments on the acts of its officials —is doing its best to create disloyalty and bring about the downfall of the British rule. What a contrast to the officials in India are those of Ceylon! The atmosphere and spirit are so different and there is such an evident and constant desire on the part of the Ceylon Government to do the best for the people and to do all things justly, and the people so happy and prosperous and loyal. One of the bright spots in India now is the administration of Madras by its present Governor, Sir Arthur Havelock, who went there from Ceylon and has won the hearts of the people. He is called there " the People's Governor." There is another man, Sir Anthony MacDonnell, the Lt.-Governor of the N.W.P., of whom the people are very fond and whose just administration has evoked wonderful outbursts of affection. The other Governors are nearly useless; yet it is so easy to rule the people and win their hearts. Thank God Ceylon is not under the India Office!

* * * * *

Light from the East

Swami Vivekánanda's books are among the best and most helpful I know in any European language. If you have not got them, you should get his *Raja Yoga*, *Bhakti Yoga* and *Karma Yoga*, and the collection of his European, Indian and American lectures. *Raja Yoga* and *Bhakti Yoga* you will like very much. In connection with the second, read Sturdy's translation of the *Narada Sutras on Love*.

* * * * *

Last November, in the course of my wanderings, I found myself in Ramesvaram, the great temple near Tannuben, and in July I spent three or four happy days in Kaltaragam, a shrine near Hambanlota, and very inaccessible and far from the haunts of men. One's neighbours are wild elephants and bears and some savage men; and two holy men. One of them (Kesopuri Swami) is just now in Colombo and I have seen a good deal of him. He has lived 70 years at Kaltaragam and is, I should think, quite 120. He came here when about 50 from Benares, and appears to have eaten some medicine whose effect will last, he thinks, about 120 years. "Death dare not approach me till then." Quite an interesting man—and of such child-like simplicity and purity. It is a great privilege to come across such men and be of some little help to them.

COLOMBO.
5th August, 1900.

DEAREST CARPENTER,

. . . I often think of my dear old grandmother, left a widow at fourteen, with two little children, surrounded by enemies thirsting for her blood and her wealth, and how alone she faced and overcame all obstacles and enemies, and brought up my uncle, Sir Coomara Swamy, and my mother, and then my brothers and myself and so many others, men and women, who are useful and leading members of Ceylon society. Alone she did it, and she could not read or write a word of her own language.

Light from the East

The 31st ult. was the anniversary of the Master's departure and was duly celebrated with the usual annual *puja* and feeding of the poor. I shall keep this letter open to enclose a little of the sacred ashes that I expect daily from them.

* * * * *

During the last years of her life, she (my grandmother) got her husband a second wife and lived in the same house, attending to her domestic duties and to the Master's wants as far as she could from her house. Ten days before his passing away, she obtained her husband's and mother-in-law's consent to go to the Swami's Monastery and nurse him, and stayed there till the end and till all the ceremonies were over—and then lay down and died. She is buried in *Samádhi*,[1] next the Master, and receives the same divine worship.

[1] For explanation of *Samddhi*, see chapter on the *Lingam*, p. 106.

Letters of P. Arunáchalam

KURUNÉGALA,
CEYLON.
25th August, 1900.

MY DEAR C.,
Happening to be here on official business, I went this morning (as I usually do when here) up the Great Rock behind the Kachcheri, and spent two happy hours thinking of the Master and you, and yearning for that Freedom which was Rishi Suka's (according to the extracts I sent you). Being still in this prison of Time, Space and Causation, Kurunégala is very dear to me—the dearest on Earth—because the Master and you stayed there with me; and I cannot help sending you a scrawl.

The D.J.'s house (district judge) is there as ever, but no trace of your leafy hermitage. Plants which I planted have grown into big shady trees, with gay flowers. I can hardly believe I have been out of the place. The old Arachchi is no longer to be seen. I fancy he has gone to his village " en pension." Gentle soul ! where shall we find his like again ? [1]

Sitting on the Rock—and with the beautiful lake and fields and gardens spread out below, I missed the boy-priest with his yellow robes, and his begging bowl in hand, walking down the hill with stately steps, and followed by his faithful attendant.[2] A very old man, bending under a load of firewood which he was carrying to market from the forest above, reminded one of olden days. There has been a slight, very slight, increase of vegetation on the bare Rock in the decade. Perhaps it will be all covered when you and I re-visit these scenes two or three centuries hence. I cannot forget your break-neck attempts at *nishtai* [3] on the slippery hill-side among the over-

---

[1] This Arachchi was a very dear and gentle old servant who used to wait on us at meals.—E. C.

[2] In the East every one down to the smallest urchin has a faithful attendant !

[3] *Nishtai*—" end," " perfection." See Sanskrit dictionary. Or at times as an adjective, "intent on," " devoted to." Kurunégala " the Elephant Rock " was a frequent resort of ours at that time.

hanging branches, and how once I was quite alarmed at your delay in coming home to breakfast. . . . How shall I forget too the gracious Master and his walks along the country roads, and discourses there; and in the house, whose ceiling was such a battleground for rats and snakes; and that walk up the Rock with him and you—and we so outdistanced by him and so fatigued, and he so fresh and pouring forth living words! It is well to have such a reminiscence to treasure up, of those happy months. Only one regret remains—and how keen I can hardly tell of it. He caught there the fatal fever, and his bodily presence and inspiration were lost to us. . . . The Railway, which you and I and others laboured to press on the Government, is now a fact, and a very paying one. The station is quite close to the Master's bungalow, and the neighborhood is much changed in consequence.

The Boer invasion of Ceylon has begun. Already, about 250 prisoners of war have

Light from the East

arrived, and we shall soon have in all about 5,000. They will be lodged in camps near Bandarawela (in Uva) and near Bentota (in Galle). Europeans and other beefeaters are already complaining of the rise in the price of beef!

    Your affectionate friend,
        P. A.

   CENSUS OFFICE,
    COLOMBO.
     February 1901.

Yours of the 23rd November received. I have been carrying it about with me for many weeks; but now I am able to answer, being detained in my office by an unexpected shower of rain.[1] . . . I think I told you I had left the Registrar-General's department some months ago . . . I am working hard at the Census. The organisation is now complete—also the preliminary Census. The final Census will be next Friday (1st March) and then we shall have cart-loads of

[1] A. was now busy with the organisation of the Census for Ceylon.—E. C.

schedules to tabulate and abstract, and make necessary matter for the Report. We have adopted new methods of enumeration, also the Bavarian Slip System of abstraction; and altogether I hope it will be a great success.

Side by side with this and my domestic interests and cares (heavy enough with a large family and limited means, but rich also in compensation of happiness beyond my desert) I keep a little corner in my soul for the seed of the Master to grow, so I manage to keep myself fairly alive and fresh. When shall I be able to say:—

"I have sought and found Him,
Him whom Vishnu and Brahma sought and found not—
Him, the Lord, yea *within myself*—
I have sought and found Him."

Your article on "Empire in India and Elsewhere" is excellent. I wonder if England will ever realise the terrible condition of India, and try to make amends. *What* a jewel in the crown of England!—famine-stricken, perishing India! Yet one of the things that makes me not despondent about England is that *there* still is a small minority of good men not afraid to tell the truth and struggle for the right. And while such men are produced, the nation cannot be quite rotten. . . . I have not seen Parama Guru Swami for several months.[1] The last time his friends tried to communicate with him, they failed. He was in India but his address not known—he having retired into the Caves and Silence.

Kind regards to your sisters and your brother Alfred.

P. A.

BRINDABANA, WAGA,
CEYLON.
29th Aug., 1917.

MY DEAR FRIEND,

You must forgive me for my long silence. But you are seldom out of my

[1] This Parama Guru (transcendent Teacher) Swami was a Guru of whom Arunáchalam often spoke—who had lived long years in the wild woods and among the animals, and to whom Arunáchalam was much attached, though seldom seen.

Letters of P. Arundchalam

thoughts and I wish my *hands* could be as devoted to you. The spirit indeed is willing, but the task of writing is very irksome. I am here on my plantation for the weekend and write in full view, from my windows, of a fine panorama of hills, covered with coco-palm and rubber, Adam's Peak in the distance, a stream at the bottom of my hill crossed by a small railway bridge not far from the station, and a glorious sky and sunshine, and a cool breeze and birds singing. I wish you could be transported here and I could have your company and talk in this peaceful spot.

I enjoyed your autobiography immensely and am glad to hear it has passed through more than one edition. I am very sorry that the collection I had made and treasured of your letters to me has disappeared. I intended to have sent them to you to refresh your memory for the autobiography. It is a great loss to me personally.

I have got entangled in various social and political activities, and have not had

Light from the East

the rest I looked forward to when I retired from the Civil Service. What with the general mismanagement by the Government, resulting in frightful oppression and misery during the years 1915 and 1916—crowds of innocent people shot down like game—and with the hoped-for spirit of liberty brought on by the war, politics loom much in view. I think I sent you copy of an address I delivered on Our Political Needs, which has led to the formation of the Ceylon Reform League. We have formulated our demands to the Secretary of State, and mean to persevere till we get them. We are preparing a memorial to the House of Commons and mean also to tackle Montagu when he comes to India. The Indian Governments, since Hardinge's departure, are going on from bad to worse, with suppressions and internments and all kinds of foolery. Fortunate for India and the Empire, Montagu's taking Chamberlain's place and making conciliatory declarations and coming out to carry into effect substantial

Letters of P. Arunáchalam

reforms! I think I sent you also reports of Social Service work we have been doing. Then we are trying to do something for the resuscitation of Tamil literature (which is greatly neglected in the rage for English) and for the safeguarding of some of the spiritual atmosphere of the East against the material Western civilisation—divorced both from Christianity and from humanity—which is destroying itself before our eyes. The Asuras (Titans) and Rakshasas of our legends must have been of the same type of civilisation; and after long periods of splendour must have come, like these modern nations, to utter grief, and remain in the race-memory only as a warning. The only hopeful thing about the present war is the refusal of the Russian people to fight—and I do hope the common people of all countries will do likewise. In no other way will this slaughter cease, unless you could get together all the " statesmen " and capitalists and the rest of the ruling classes (who sit at home at ease, and send out the youth

Light from the East

in their millions to be slaughtered) and dispose of *them* somehow. It is difficult for us here to know what is really going on in Europe, as the outspoken papers are not allowed to come here. Financial distress is becoming acute here, owing to want of freight to send our produce abroad and to lack of money. But it serves everybody right for being so dependent on the foreigner and not on ourselves. The whole system is rotten.

* * * *
* * *

The daughter we lost was not Maheswari, but her sister Manourmani—a sweet child and the pet of all who knew her. Why a good God allows such misery to be caused is not intelligible. Why, indeed, does he permit the agonies of millions in this war? What a sorry scheme of things. In the

Letters of P. Arunáchalam

case of my dear daughter, whose bright young life was nipped in the bud, I sometimes think the explanation may be that her brief sojourn here was necessary for her to work out her development and pass into a fuller, richer life. "Her flower-feet," says a Tamil poet of a woman's soft and delicate tread, "touched the earth lightly like the lives of those who are born to make up the deficiencies (of a past life)." It has been the greatest sorrow of my life. Though two years have passed, I think of her daily. Last night I saw her in her purity and beauty and was so happy embracing her. It was but "a moment's ornament," alas! But enough of this sadness.

In Tamil poetry, in which I often seek relief from my thoughts, one comes across images of the vault of heaven compared to a sea or lake, with clouds as waves or foam, stars as fish, the moon as a lotus, the crescent moon as a boat, etc. I don't remember such images in Western poetry. I wonder if you can think of any. Here are some

Light from the East

passages, but the beauty of the original is lost in translation.

"O round white moon, that lighteth the heavens all night long, tell poor desolate me one word. Hast thou seen him, that rogue who wooed and won me amid the young laurel, the pines alone my witness?"

This idea is amplified elsewhere.

"O moon-lotus, blossoming full round and white—putting to shame the flower-faces of heavenly maidens and shedding ambrosial honey—in the cool, celestial lake, where cloud-weeds rise dark stemmed from the sea and spread on every side and star-fish leap, where purple clouds—old foam—and white clouds—new foam—rise in beauty and scatter everywhere, and the Ganges (the Milky Way) rushes resistless through many months, O moon, I weak and fainting have one poor request to make of thee," etc.

The love-lorn lady is here the Soul seeking the Lord.

Similar similes occur in an address of her friend and confidante exhorting her to worship the young moon.

"Fold thy fair hands, dark-eyed maid, in worship unto the little, white, soft-rayed crescent moon that showeth in the twilight sky like unto the crescent on the matted locks of Him that standeth in glory in Tillai, His golden feet a refuge for my safety and a guard against my seeking, even unawares, other and false gods."

The crescent moon is also compared to the tusk of a celestial elephant.

"The pure white curved tusk on the face of the star-spotted sky-elephant, whose breath is the blowing wind, whose trickling mist is the rain, whose side bells are the rising and the setting sun."

Yesterday, while watching a big elephant rooting out some of my rubber trees in a plantation which I am thinning, I thought the simile rather good. The elephant, being unfamiliar to the Western poet, would not occur to him. It would be strange if the other similes did *not* occur to him.

Now I must be done, as my head and hand ache. May the "Hun" be merciful and spare the ship that carries this to you! Remember me affectionately to your sisters and, brother Alfred and to your comrade George. Where now is that portrait Rothenstein made of you? Was it a good one?

Light from the East

Did you see those he made of me, one at Benares and one at his house in the country? I would like to get photos of them, if I knew where they were. Remember me to him [1] also if you write. I have not heard from him for a long time, nor written to him, being, as you know, a very bad correspondent. But I must write. He is such a dear chap. The last I heard of him was from Mrs. Woods, widow of the Master of the Temple.

    Ever yours affectionately,
        P. ARUNÁCHALAM.

---

[1] Rothenstein.

SUPPLEMENT TO
LIGHT FROM THE EAST

CONSISTING OF FOUR ESSAYS OR ARTICLES ON

		PAGE
1. THE LINGAM AND SENSUAL DESIRE	. . . .	87
2. THE ENDEAVOUR TO CONTROL DESIRE	. . .	109
3. BIRTH-CONTROL AND BISEXUALITY	. . .	126
4. THE MOUNA SWAMIS AND THE ANIMALS	. .	143

THE LINGAM & SENSUAL DESIRE

I WISH to-day to write about the word *Lingam*, which plays so important a part in the Sanskrit language and which corresponds to something very important in actual life. The word in modern times has become so much used that almost everyone knows its meaning. The Sanskrit Lexicon gives the word *link* as closely related to it, and I do not suppose one could find a better general word than that. The *lingam* is primarily *the link*, i.e. the organ which acts as link between the two sexes—but, needless to say, it has many derivative significations. It indicates, of course, the physical tie between man and woman, and as such every one understands its meaning and importance. The two great divisions of the human race—complementary to each other as they are—are held together by the

Light from the East

lingam. It is the power which practically makes mankind one and which compels its two great sections into one fellowship.

There are very numerous *lingams* (conventional representations of the male organ) to be seen, scores and scores of them, in the arcades and cloisters of the Hindu Temples, and to these women of all classes, especially those who wish to become mothers, resort, anointing them copiously with oil, and signalising their respect and devotion to them in a very practical way. And the *lingam* representing the male organ (in some form or other, as upright stone or pillar or obelisk or slender round tower) occurs all over the world, notably in Ireland, and forms such a memorial of the adoration paid by early folk to the great emblem and instrument of human fertility as cannot be mistaken. The pillars set up by Solomon in front of his temple were obviously from their names, Jachin and Boaz,[1] signs of the same character;

---

[1] " He shall establish " (i.e. stand up) and " in him is strength" are the marginal references in our Bible.

The Lingam and Sensual Desire

and the fact that they were crowned with pomegranates (the universal symbol of the female) confirms and clinches this interpretation.

"It is pretty clear indeed that the early peoples saw in Sex the great cohesive force which kept the Tribe together and sustained the Race. In the early stage of Simple Consciousness this must have been one of the first things that the budding intellect perceived. Sex became one of the earliest divinities, and there is abundant evidence that its organs and processes generally were invested with a religious sense of awe and sanctity. The lingam was, in fact, the symbol (or rather the actuality) of the permanent undying life of the race. And whatever taboos may have among different peoples guarded its operations, it was essentially a thing to be honoured and not to be concealed or ashamed of. Rather the contrary. For instance, the early Christian writer, Hippolytus, Bishop of Pontus, who was a pillar of the Church (A.D. 200), in his *Refutation of all Heresies*, Book V, says that the Samothracian Mysteries celebrate Adam as the primal or archetypal Man eternal in the heavens; and that "Habitually there stand in the temple of the Samothracians two images of naked men having their *pudenda* turned upwards, as is also the case with the statue of Mercury on Mount Cyllene. And the aforesaid images are figures of the primal man, and of that spiritual one that is born again, in every respect of the same substance with that (first) man."

Light from the East

It is interesting to note that this Father of the Church (Hippolytus) evidently believed in the existence of a Divine Being, the primal Man, the root and origin of Creation, from whom indeed Creation continually flows, and who continually renews his sustaining activity therein. Thus the adoration of the *lingam* in early times appears as perfectly natural, and indeed a fundamental part both of religion and philosophy. This primal Being was the original anointed One, or Christ,[1] after whom earthly kings were named and who gave to the latter their authority. The anointing of the Lingam itself was a very obvious and practical expedient, which in time became the original source of very wide spread customs and ceremonies. Over these, however, we need not at present delay.

G. R. S. Mead, in his *Thrice-Greatest Hermes*, speaks of the Christos, the Anointed One, as being "a revelation of the Mystery of Man," and speaks further of Attis as

[1] *Christos*, of course, *means* "Anointed."

The Lingam and Sensual Desire

abandoning his sex in the worship of the mother-goddess (*Dea Syria*) and so ascending to Heaven—" a new man Male-Female, and the origin of all things: the hidden Mystery being the phallus (or Lingam) itself, which was commonly erected as Hermes in all roads and boundaries and temples—the Conductor and Re-conductor of Souls." This passage about the New Man, who is represented as both Male and Female and the conductor and re-conductor of Souls, is especially interesting.

Only lately, in collaboration with my friend Mr. G. C. Barnard (writing under the name of Barnefield), we have published a book on *The Poet Shelley*,[1] in which the remarkable combination is pointed out of masculine and feminine attributes in Shelley's case.

"This idea of a double sex, or of a bisexual temperament,[2] clearly haunted the minds of early peoples, and

[1] *The Psychology of the Poet Shelley* (published by Allen & Unwin).
[2] Which is also frequent among the Italians of to-day.

Light from the East

I have suggested (*Intermediate Types*, p. 82) that this idea may date, not only from the fact that the sex-temperament in its earliest form *is* undifferentiated, but also from the fact that the great leaders of mankind have so often shown this fusion in themselves. The feminine traits in genius (as in a Shelley or a Byron) are well marked in the present day. We have only to go back to the Persian Bâb of the last century, or to a St. Francis, or even to a Jesus of Nazareth, to find the same traits present in founders and leaders of religious movements in historical times. And it becomes easy to suppose the same again of those early figures—who once probably were men—those Apollos, Buddhas, Dionysus, Osiris and so forth—to suppose that they, too, were somewhat bisexual in temperament, and that it was really largely owing to that fact that they were endowed with far-reaching powers and became leaders of mankind" (*Psychology of the Poet Shelley*, pp. 44 and 45).

Through all this we dimly forebode the emergence of an ideal of the human being somewhat different from that usually accepted. If the male and the female, through a long period of estrangement, have become in the present day divorced from each other, they have both suffered ; they have both missed some of the treasures of life. But we

The Lingam and Sensual Desire

dimly forebode in the future a return and a restoration. If love, relegated to heaven, had so far become a merely philosophical, pious and spiritual affair; and if sex, remaining on Earth, but deserted by the redeeming presence, had, as a matter of fact, fallen into mere " carnal curiosity and wretchlessness of unclean living," there remained obviously no remedy but the bringing of the two together again, the reconciliation of the physical and the spiritual and (after many sufferings) the reunion of Eros and Psyche. That, then, *is destined to take place*. Eros and Psyche will be restored to each other to build again the perfect human being.

I may here quote from *Pagan and Christian Creeds*, page 250:—

"The truth is that the second stage of human psychologic evolution—that stage especially connected with the fall of Man—is an aberration, a divorce, a parenthesis. With its culmination and dismissal the Man passes back into the simple state of union with the Whole. (The state of Ekágratá in the Hindu philosophy—one pointedness, singleness of mind). And the consciousness of the Whole, and of things past and things to come and things far around—which consciousness had been shut out by the concentration on the local self—begins to return again.

"With the mention of *Ekágratá* we now come back to my friend Arunáchalam's letters and the subject of Gñanam. Whether Gñanam as a Philosophy contemplated any such further evolution of humanity as here suggested, I know not. It is, perhaps, a defect of the general doctrines of Gñanam that in them evolution and the modern ideas of gradual change and expansion are left out of account, and the system takes on a somewhat fixed and stationary form which does not allow of *Growth*, and does not include evolution. This, to my mind, is a serious drawback. Still it is better, perhaps, at present to call attention to the many vital and helpful conceptions which are actually at work in Gñanam—as that is the special object of this paper—and leave its defects for consideration on some future occasion.

"Gñanam speaks of a universal, pure, absolute consciousness, shining everywhere, though not always equally evident to our perception, and permeating and vitalising all, from a tuft of grass to the highest deity.[1] It is Siva Sambandam, the god who bands (or binds) all together and from whom none may escape. He is the Dancing God—the dance symbolising the operations of the Universe. 'In the innermost shrine of the great

[1] The *Letters*.

The Lingam and Sensual Desire

temple at Chidambaram (in the south of India) is the image of Siva in the attitude of a dancer. Immediately behind the sacred image hangs a curtain which screens off the Holy of Holies. To look behind the curtain is a privilege rarely accorded. But the mercenary priests can be induced to make exceptions; and some years ago, and again on this visit (says Arunáchalam), I was granted the privilege. What do you think I saw behind the curtain? Emptiness—mere space. I did not understand it on my first visit—nor do the priests. But the thing is clear to me now as explained by the Guru, and so I find it explained in the books. The essence of Saivam, as I have said, is *Equality*. This is typified by the space behind the curtain, but Equality is not confined, as among the Westerners, to human beings (or should I say *white* men?), but embraces all living things as well as the things called *not* living—called so because the Divine Consciousness in them is not apparent to our coarser senses. Equality underlies the dance in the Universe, as in the temple-worship it underlies the ritual.'"

The idea here suggested that mere empty Space is a symbol of Equality is a fertile and important one. Space indeed is a very beautiful thing, as all artists know. It conveys the sense of freedom—freedom to move in any direction. It implies the promise and the possibility of new life and develop-

Light from the East

ment, of existence unshackled, pointing the way to Paradise, giving room for growth and expansion. "Life is a poor miserable affair," says the author of the *Letters*, "unless it is regarded as a training-ground for the soul—a place where the soul may, by worthily discharging its duties and experiencing its sorrows and joys, purify itself and gain a knowledge of and *become* its true self, "God" —i.e. become indeed *akása*, the life which is the freedom of the Universe.

But I am speaking here especially of the Lingam, and the following passage from A.'s letter from Tanjore (of the 27th July, 1896) gives an impressive idea of the honour in which this emblem is held, even down to to-day, among people uncorrupted by the suspicions and antagonisms of "Civilisation":—

"I am here on a few days' leave—the first holiday I have had for five and a half years. I came here to attend the anniversary *puja* or religious ceremony in commemoration of the Master's departure. The ceremony took place on the 23rd inst.—the normal ceremonies that occur in the temple of Siva on grand occasions—

The Lingam and Sensual Desire

together with the feeding of over a thousand persons. On the site where his body is interred is a Lingam [1]

[1] One can easily understand how, in early days, when everything strange or unexplained took on a mystic character, the organ in question lent itself to magical beliefs. The placing of a *lingam* at the spot where the holy man's body was interred was, I take it, a relic of some *very ancient rite* which delighted to honour, in the departed member of the Tribe, the emblem of his immortal life. For the *lingam*, as I have already explained, *was* the symbol of the solidarity and persistence of the Tribe— the great human Fellowship—and accordingly the worship of the Lingam did, as a matter of fact, spread widely over the world. The organ became the symbol of the Primal Man, eternal in the Heavens—as in the quotation from Hippolytus given above; and its adoption may perhaps be taken as prophetic of a new type of Man (or Woman) already appearing in our midst—a type which is destined to unite the qualities of both sexes (the tenderness and adaptability of the female with the strength and reliability of the male) and to be a herald of the reunion of Eros and Psyche.

For indeed the perfected Consciousness (which arises from the blending of the male and female types) has, as suggested in the *Letters*, a divine quality resembling the pervasive quality of the Ether; and Space—the ordinary three-dimensional space—thus figures as the training-ground of the Soul—a region in which, meeting with endless experiences and changes, the soul learns to say to itself in each case (like Svetaketu in the Khandogya Upanishad) "Thou art That, Thou art That," and again "Thou art That." Identifying itself thus with all things, the soul is able to pass through the world like a bird through the air, making use always of the medium in which it moves, but encountering neither solid resistance nor serious obstacle.

Again, the Lingam is said to be the Conductor and Reconductor

Light from the East

to which the worship is offered as to the Master. It is remarkable to note the piety and reverence of the crowd. The Master's widow was also there—a gentle, gracious lady, full of love and kindness, and still the support and comfort of the whole household, including the vagrant Samanathan's family; the latter still rebellious and fighting and unhappy in his soul, but very interesting and learned—and destined no doubt to win peace in the end; for Tillaináyaka Swami has blessed him. The younger brother, Soma-sundurampillai, takes after the Master— very practical and sensible and helpful—and bravely bears the burden of the family, not forgetting the daily prayer to the Master. The Samadhi building is a simple brick building, thatched with coco-nut leaf and situated in an acre of ground, which his energy has converted into a garden from which flowers and fruits and water are obtained for the worship.

The editor of the *Letters* hopes that these few notes, casual and scattered though they are, may help to throw light on various points

of souls, from which I gather that the early people thought— and perhaps with reason—that the tiny organisms which we call *spermatozoa* were indeed souls, and the seeds of countless bodies speeding on their magic errands through Nature.

It also figured as the link between the generations and as the pledge and assurance of our Common Life, and in somewhat the same sense as a fitting token to be laid on a grave.

The Lingam and Sensual Desire

connected with Gñanam; and he will, in conclusion, run through the subject again with the more special object of bringing it into touch with modern Thought. It will be seen that the conception of God as Siva Sambandam is in truth (allowing for change of terms) a very modern one. It is the conception of a God who encloses and *is* all Creation—" in whom we live and move and have our being "—it is a conception somewhat pantheistical no doubt, but very much in line with the conclusions of latter-day science. It accentuates the opinion that the whole of creation is bound together in one organism from which no single part can be abstracted without altering or modifying the rest. *Sambandam*, i.e. " bound in one piece." And this links on with the doctrine of Akása, which certainly corresponds to the Western belief in the existence of an all-pervading Ether—except that *our* Ether is a thing devoid of intelligence, whereas the Akása alluded to—certainly under the form of Gñana-akása—is penetrated with intelligence throughout and is the form under which all intelligent beings are already understood to be in touch with each other. It assumes a solidarity of Intelligence throughout the Universe, and something corresponding to the " Cosmic Consciousness " of some modern thinkers ; and it implies the very modern conceptions of Equality and Democracy, because the true Equality and the true Democracy *mean* the overpassing of barriers between cliques and classes and individuals, and the discovery of the common ground on which all may meet. The sense of Equality makes freedom of movement possible because, wherever one may go, there is seen to be a common ground of life and a common bond of interest ; the barriers are abolished in advance, and the consequent sense of Liberation becomes one of the most precious acquisitions of the human Spirit.

Closely allied to " Equality " is the power which in Gñanam is frequently honoured under the name *Ekágratá*, or one pointedness (*Eká*, one, and *gratá*, a point)—the

The Lingam and Sensual Desire

power of holding the mind concentrated on one point at a time. The importance of this habit, this power, can hardly be overestimated. We are so accustomed to let the mind wander and ramble from point to point that we are hardly conscious of the resulting damage to the thinking faculty and its consequent loss of true penetration and power; but there it is, and it is often only when the mind throws off this deadly habit that it wakes to the consciousness of its own real virtue, and of the sad waste that has been going on during the period of its distraction. *Ekâ gratâ*, one pointedness, almost perforce carries with it the meaning of *penetration*. If a tool is to penetrate, it must, at any rate during the period of its use, be concentrated on one point. It is not meant that it must always be concentrated on the *same* point. That would be almost as wasteful; but if the mind is to penetrate into and become master of any subject, it must at least have the power of sinking therein till it has reached its very

Light from the East

heart and essence. *Eká gratá* conveys therefore this idea of Penetration; and it may be noted that those who have attained this faculty are by no means lost in dreams, but are singularly able to deal with and disentangle the practical problems of life. One of the most clinging and persistent delusions belonging to our stage of evolution—though perhaps *without* it our efficiency would be much crippled—is the delusion of "I" and "Mine"—*Ahankára* (from *Aham*, I, and *Kara*, character), the "I character" of the mind. This is so deeply ingrained —as we all know—that it is one of the last things to be dismissed and got rid of. Yet it is obvious that until it is dismissed, no really accurate and truthful conclusion can be reached on any one of the problems of life. It is exactly like the old geocentric idea in Astronomy —the delusion that the Earth was the centre of the heavenly motions. As long as that obtained and was respected it was simply impossible for clear explanations of Astronomy to be arrived at. And so with the

The Lingam and Sensual Desire

delusion of our own overwhelming importance; until that delusion is scotched and despatched none of our views can be really accurate. The " I," after all, is a silly old thing, whose head is very liable to be turned ! And to exalt such an *Old Man of the Sea* into a place of domination in our lives is only to prepare for ourselves a way of worse confusion and downfall.

From that confusion we must, at all costs, shake ourselves free; the " I " is not a scientific reality. It does not actually correspond to anything in Nature. It is a mirage thrown up by our vanity; and the sooner we shake free and dismiss it the better.

In all this (as I have said before) there is much that reminds one of the manifestations of Sex in the Body—its burning, withering intensity—the fixed almost rigid condition which precedes its culmination, the threads like lightning, streaming from all parts of the organism to their fulfilment, and the ecstatic deliverance. The man

Light from the East

becomes God! No wonder that this condition has from the farthest back times been glorified as holy!

It is indeed the state of Samadhi, celebrated in all the sacred writings. People ask "What *is* Samadhi?" The answer is simple. The word explains itself. Samadhi is "sameness" (see the dictionaries). It is the state—as I think Arunáchalam indicates (see the *Letters, passim*) in which the worshipper enters into sameness with the god whom he worships.[1] It is the state in which the distinction between subject and object disappears, in which (as in Buddhism) the man passes into identity with the whole universe, and comes to understand that much misunderstood thing—the doctrine of *Nirvana*—which to three-quarters, perhaps, of the religionists of the human race represents

[1] It is *very remarkable* how this identification occurs and recurs in all sorts of ancient and primitive cults (see *Pagan and Christian Creeds*, pp. 108, 109, etc.) and among rude peoples whom one would not a priori have supposed capable of any philosophic speculation. This fact enables us to understand how early peoples understood many things of which *we* are ignorant.

The Lingam and Sensual Desire

(even though they do not understand it) the *ne plus ultra* of salvation. It is that root-condition in which there *is* no Self to disturb or destroy the realisation of the world's perfection; but in which the light of the latter shines, clear and unclouded—whether for a moment or whether indeed for a millennium.

As I say, the references to this condition in the sacred writings of the human race are *endless*—though often enough obscure and hard to understand! And as I also say, it is passing strange that in the earliest history of Man we should find—as we *do* find—a thousand symbolic rites and ceremonies adopted and commonly in use which can only really *be* understood by reference to the same. It is a condition in which, as Arunáchalam says, there is "no Self ever bobbing up like a Jack-in-the-box, but in which the divine Light shines forth pure and serene"—as for example the following extract will help to show.

Light from the East

"At Kumbakonam, two hours by train from here, there is a great Mouna Swami (*silent* Master), who has been there over thirty years. He says and does nothing, being in a more emancipated state than even Tillaináyaka Swami, and like him, stark naked. I went there yesterday. A temple and monastery have grown round him. He is the central object of worship, a live Man-God. It was a special festival, and he was anointed [1] and worshipped with all the elaboration used on great occasions in the temple; and the assembled crowd sang and prostrated themselves before him and worshipped with even greater ardour and piety than in the temples. It was a remarkable sight.[2] He showed not the least trace, through the many hours, of intelligence of what was going on. His eyes were open and moved, etc., but saw nothing—they simply reflected objects like a mirror. He arose, or sat or walked when he was gently touched and pushed. There was a slight play of the fingers, and the eyes moved. That was all. External objects made no impression on his senses. *Yet it was clear that it was not a case of decay.* There was such a gracious calm and peace and glory on his face and around him. Why was he silent, quite still? The answer of one of his devotees was: "When He is all things, who is there to speak, and to whom?" It was a wonderful experience

---

[1] Here we see illustrated in quite modern times the meaning of the word *Christos* or Christ—"the Anointed One."

[2] No doubt it was! Fancy a fervent crowd of worshippers prostrating themselves before Mr. Stanley Baldwin and singing hymns to him!

The Lingam and Sensual Desire

to see such a *poojah* and to meet people from all parts of India who firmly believed in him as the Paramatma (i.e. the transcendent soul of creation) and could each tell of blessings received from him."

It is, perhaps, only in India that one could have such an experience. The whole surroundings there aid and stimulate belief in the transcendent greatness of the human soul; and the Mouna Swamis (Masters, of whom there are hundreds or perhaps thousands in the Peninsula) contribute, each in their special way, to the confirmation of that belief.

The unalloyed pure consciousness is *there*, burning and blazing in the depths; and the world which we know—the world of actual life and experience—is derived from that one by a process which we can best describe, perhaps, as a process of alloy, of watering down, or dilution (see *A Visit to a Gñani*, p. 54).

"The pure intelligence (*arivu*) is impartite spirit-space (Gñana-akása), nothing else. It becomes fettered by the thought which differentiates this body and its intellectual faculties, its experiences and spheres, as "I" and

Light from the East

" mine "; and is emancipated if that differentiation ceases " (i.e. when the motionless intelligence is realised as God).

And indeed in these days of scientific belief in an Ether filling all space, and rippling throughout with instant Intelligence, there is no particular difficulty in giving one's assent to the mystic doctrine of the Gñana-akása.

THE ENDEAVOUR TO CONTROL DESIRE

IT is probable that the tyranny of the Sex-desire has been in its way quite necessary. Nothing else, perhaps, would have forced forward that abundance (or over-abundance) of population which seems to have been a necessary condition of evolution, and of our ascent in the scale of life. Up the difficult stairs which lead to an immortal destiny, the human race has been *compelled* to climb. This sex-desire with unsparing severity has *driven* us forward; and if it has sometimes in the process proved itself a nuisance (which it certainly has) we must forgive in view of the good intentions evidently underlying! The lesson of the Axolotl, which creature (if the theory is correct) can only be transformed from a

Light from the East

water-breathing to an air-breathing animal by a strong and persistent *compulsion*, is worth consideration; and if Everest or Chomo'lhari demand months or years of preparation before they will yield to our attacks, we can hardly expect the very ancient sex-instinct (which underlies Creation and dates from the farthest back beginnings of human existence) to give way at the first onset; yet in the end (I doubt not) it will lead us on to something glorious beyond imagination.

Those who study Gñanam—and they are an increasing number—are so convinced of the folly and fatuity of encouraging the old and outworn habits of mind which circle round the words "I" and "mine" that they tend very decidedly to abandon them, feeling that their continued use does but help to strengthen their hold upon the mind and confirm its ancient prejudices. The Gñanis, for instance, do as a rule avoid these words, and pass by them as quickly and with as little ceremony as may be; but

The Endeavour to Control Desire

the "Jack-in-the-box" is not so easily put down. It has a habit of springing up at inconvenient moments; and quite a time may elapse before its ways are effectively altered.

Vi-deka-mukti[1] is the expression for deliverance from the tyrannical habits of the body, and this is the prayer which is often in the mouth of the student of Gñanam. However foolish the old order may be, its power cannot be broken at once, and a certain amount of patience and perseverance in the good work of freeing oneself are found to be quite necessary. *Vi-deka-mukti.* Strange that it should ever have entered into the hearts of human beings thus to transform themselves—for that is what they are in reality trying to do—to effect a transformation, a transfiguration of their ordinary nature. Yet it must be remembered that one of the most common events of our public and general life is just that—what is called

[1] *Deka*, the body; *mukti*, freedom; *Vi*, possibly from an original *dvi*, meaning "in two parts." See Monier-Williams, *Sanskrit-English Dictionary*.

Light from the East

conversion—as when a drunkard suddenly becomes a teetotaller, or a profane and foul-mouthed talker a pious Bible-reader. The thing *happens*—whatever the explanation may be—and in such cases the habits and inner nature of the person are changed.

If the *axolotl*, the Mexican Eft, can be transformed from a water-breathing to an air-breathing animal by persistent pressure and compulsion in that direction; why something of a similar kind *may* be true with regard to the *Lingam* of which we have been speaking. It may be that we have by no means yet found for the latter its perfect and permanent function.

The story of the agelong and determined struggle of mankind against the generative instinct is one which at present we can only trace in barest outline, and whose ultimate meaning and rational conclusion we cannot possibly foresee, yet some meaning and some conclusion it must surely have.

It is a common saying that the *protozoa*—

The Endeavour to Control Desire

those tiny creatures that consist of only one cell—are immortal. In a sense it is true that they do not die. For though thousands of them may perish (and are constantly perishing) yet their line of life from one generation to another does not perish. On the contrary it branches ever into new forms. From some original protozoon down through thousands of generations, even to the latest product of animal or human evolution, the line of descent has remained continuous. But the latest form is so far different from the earliest that it would indeed be hard at a glance to trace their connection. The life then being in reality continuous and so long-enduring should surely be regarded as *one* life, capable of almost indefinite modification and expansion :—

"For as with the first blossoming of self-consciousness in the human mind, came the dawn of an immense cycle of human experience—a cycle indeed of exile from Eden, of suffering and toil and blind wanderings in the wilderness, yet a cycle absolutely necessary and unavoidable—so now the redemption, the return, the restoration has to come through another forward step in the same domain. Abandoning the quest and the glorification of the separate isolated self, we have to return to the cosmic universal life. It is the blossoming indeed of this 'new life' in the deeps of our minds which *is* salvation, and which all the expressions which I have just cited have indicated. It is this presence which all down the ages has been hailed as Saviour and Liberator; the day-break of a consciousness so much vaster, so much more glorious, than all that has gone before, that the little candle of the local self is swallowed up in its rays. It is the return home, the return into direct touch with Nature and Man—the liberation from the long exile of separation, from the painful sense of isolation and the odious nightmare of guilt and 'sin.' Can we doubt that this new birth—this third stage of consciousness, if we like to call it so—has to come, that it is indeed not merely a pious hope or a tentative theory, but a *fact* testified to already by a cloud of witnesses in the past—witnesses shining in their own easily recognisable and authentic light—yet for the most part isolated from each other among the arid and unfruitful wastes of Civilisation, like glow-worms in the dry grass of a summer night." [1]

Since the first dim evolution of human self-consciousness an immense period—perhaps 30,000 years, perhaps even more—has elapsed. Now, in the present day, this

[1] See *Pagan and Christian Creeds*, p. 236.

The Endeavour to Control Desire

period is reaching its culmination, and though it will not terminate immediately, its end is, so to speak, in sight.

"And not only does the Third Stage bring illumination, intuitive understanding of processes in Nature and Humanity, sympathy with the animals, artistic capacity and so forth, but it necessarily brings a new Order of Society. A preposterous—one may almost say a hideous—social Age is surely drawing to its end. The *débâcle* which we are witnessing to-day all over Europe (including the British Islands), the break-up of old institutions, the generally materialistic outlook on life, the coming to the surface of huge masses of diseased and fatuous populations, the scum and dregs created by the past order—all point to the end of a Dispensation. Protestantism and Commercialism, in the two fields of religion and daily life have, as I have indicated before, been occupied in concentrating the mind of each man solely on his *own* welfare, the salvation of his *own* soul or body. These two forces have therefore been disruptive to the last degree ; they mark the culmination of the Self-conscious Age—a culmination in War, Greed, Materialism, and the general principle of *Devil take the hindmost*—and the clearing of the ground for the new order which is to come. So there is hope for the human race. Its evolution is not all a mere formless craze and jumble. There is an inner necessity by which Humanity unfolds from one degree or plane of consciousness to another. And if there has been a great 'Fall' or Lapse into conflict and disease and 'sin' and misery, occupying the major part of the Historical period hitherto, we see that this period is only brief, so to speak, in comparison with the whole curve of growth and expansion.[1] We see also that, as I have said before, the belief in a state of salvation or deliverances has in the past ages never left itself quite without a witness in the creeds and rituals and poems and prophecies of mankind. Class rule has been the mark of this second period of human evolution and has inevitably given birth during that period to wars and self-aggrandisement of classes and sections, and their consequent greeds and tyrannies over other classes and sections. It is not found in the primitive human tribes and societies, and will not be found in the final forms of human association. The liberated and emancipated Man will pass unconstrained and unconstraining through all grades and planes of human fellowship, equal and undisturbed, and never leaving his true home and abiding-place in the heart of all."

In the Earl of Ronaldshay's very interesting book entitled, *Lands of the Thunder-*

---

[1] See Dr. R. M. Bucke's *Cosmic Consciousness* (Dutton & Co., New York), which book may be obtained, complete, from Mr. Watkins, 21, Cecil Court, Charing Cross Road, W.C., for 25s. net. The words "for war and the weapons of war" are, I believe, not found in the earliest human writings (see *Pagan and Christian Creeds*, p. 229).

The Endeavour to Control Desire

bolt (Sikhim, Chumbi, and Bhutan), there are some passages which I may quote as bearing on the present subject. The author says, speaking of India's " absorbing and eternal quest " (p. 148) :—

"The subject was brought to the fore again by our encounter with the presiding Lama of the Lachen gompa, a spiritual leader of such eminence and reputation as to have earned for himself the title of Gompchen, or Great Hermit. Over a period of twenty-six years he had been in the habit of retiring from the world from time to time and living a life of solitary meditation in a remote cave, the situation of which was pointed out to us later, high up and difficult of access, among the cliffs of an inhospitable tract of mountain above the path to Thangu. One of these periodic retirements from the world has been protracted over a period of five years, during which time he had seen no human being and had kept body and soul together on a minimum of food. . . . From conversation with him (the Lama) it appeared that he had reached the stage of Arahatship, and was therefore beyond good and evil. . . . He admitted quite frankly that the vain repetitions, the images upon the altars, the *mandalas* and all the elaborate externalism of Lamaism as ordinarily practised meant nothing to him at all. . . . Before parting I asked him the question which King Milinda asked the Sage Nagasena, namely, would he be reborn or would he at the close of his present life attain

Light from the East

Nirvana? He replied that this was a very big question, the answer to which was not easy to give. The fact that Nirvana was within his grasp was not in doubt. He was the sole arbiter of his future destiny. But it might be that at the hour of death, out of pity for the sufferings of humanity, he might decide to be born once more in order to extend his saving help to others. . . . All that was said on the subject was clearly spoken in all seriousness. Did this Tibetan priest—to all outward appearance a man differing little from the generality of mankind—believe implicitly all that he said? It is difficult to say. This, at least, is certain, the motive which impels men to leave their fellows and for years on end, spurning the weaknesses of the flesh, to live a life of solitary confinement, must be an extraordinarily powerful one. The two lamas of my experience commanding the deepest and most widespread veneration are, undoubtedly, the Gompchen of Lachen and the learned principal of the Tung Kar Monastery in Chumbi, the Geshi Tromo. In each case knowledge and wisdom have been sought in solitary communing with the spirit,[1] during long periods of confinement in remote fastnesses in the mountains cut off from the haunts of men. It was with every sign of awe and reverence that I was told how, high on the rugged sides of Cho-mo-lhari, the Geshi Tromo had sought to wrest from the great unknown something of the secret of the universe."

[1] This, I imagine, could only prove successful by steady and persistent suppression of Thought over long periods.—E. C.

The Endeavour to Control Desire

Up in the snows of the vast Himahlya mountains—not far indeed from the region which our explorers have lately invaded, there have from time immemorial dwelt such hermits whose one idea has been—not to ascend Everest or Chomolhari—but to scale heights even more difficult than these—to dominate and overcome the foundational instinct of the human race, the instinct of sexual congress.

What is the meaning of this and countless similar facts ? That the instinct can be extirpated I do not for a moment suppose ; but that its functioning may be and will be *modified*, profoundly modified, I regard as highly probable. Similar modifications are the very material of Evolution, and so in the modern sense are they the material of Creation itself.

We are stumbling, it will be seen, into the contemplation of enormous periods of time. These stages of consciousness—including not only the psychology of the Animals —a subject with which I hope to deal presently—but also the growth of *self*-consciousness, the consequent exile from Eden, the redemption through entry into another form of consciousness (the cosmic consciousness)—all imply the lapse of centuries or millenniums. Dr. Bucke insists that the whole human race has to rise into this New Order, and *that* (to use a slang expression) is a big order! Yet the fact that the periods of time implied are so great constitutes no reason for ignoring the same. Twenty centuries ago (about the second century B.C.) we find very similar problems being discussed. There was, every year at Eleusis, a solemn and lengthy procession or pilgrimage made, symbolic of the long pilgrimage of the human soul, its sufferings and deliverance. " Almost always," says Archdeacon Cheetham, " the suffering of a god—suffering followed by triumph—seems to have been the subject of the sacred drama." Then occasionally to the Neophytes, after taking part in the pilgrimage, and when their minds had been prepared by an ordeal of darkness and

The Endeavour to Control Desire

fatigue and terrors, was accorded a revelation of Paradise, and even a vision of Transfiguration—the form of the Hierophant himself, or Teacher of the Mysteries, being seen half lost in a blaze of light. (Quoted from Dr. Farnell, *Cults of the Greek States*, Vol. III.)

It is interesting to find, speaking of the illumination (φωτισμος) which was held to attend Initiation and Salvation, that Dr. Bucke, in his records of the oncoming of *Cosmic Consciousness*, speaks over and over again of the *Light*, in flashes or in more permanent brilliance, which attended these experiences; and it is impossible to suppose that these records—in the hands of a man so weighty and so careful as Dr. Bucke, and so experienced in medical matters—are mere invention or, at best, imaginations.

In one of the Orphic Tablets [1] the phrase

---

[1] These Tablets (so called) are instructions to the dead as to their passage into the other world, and have been found in the tombs in Italy and elsewhere inscribed on very thin gold plates and buried with the departed.

Light from the East

"I am a child of earth and the starry heaven, but my race is of heaven (alone)" occurs more than once; and in another the dead person himself is addressed as follows:—
"Hail thou who hast endured the suffering, such as indeed thou hadst never endured before; *thou hast become god from man!*" Ecstasy indeed was the culmination of the religious life; and, what is especially interesting to us, Salvation or the divine nature was open to *all* men—to all, that is, who should go through the necessary stages of preparation for it.

Reitzenstein contends [1] that in the Mysteries, Transfiguration, Salvation, and New Birth were often conjoined. He says that in the Egyptian Osiris-cult, the Initiate acquired a nature "equal to God" ($\mathit{\iota\sigma\acute{o}\theta\epsilon os}$), the very same expression as that used of Jesus Christ in Philippians ii, 6, etc. In all this there are many and striking parallels with Gñanam; but it is not necessary to

[1] *Die hellenistischen Mysterien-Religionen,* by R. Reitzenstein (Leipzig, 1910).

The Endeavour to Control Desire

delay over them now as the correspondences are very obvious.

That the words "I" and "mine" will have ultimately to be abandoned is sufficiently clear. Not that we need make any hard and fast rules on the subject, or invent dogmas; but simply that with the passing of the need for such words they will inevitably lose their frequency and force. We have said that in the early societies a state of Communism naturally prevailed, and I think there is little doubt but that with the further evolution of social life a similar communism will recur. Our powers of production are now so enormous that to insist on little matters of private property has already become quite old-fashioned, and it is easy to foresee a time when "property rights" will be dissolved out in a general condition of affluence and well-being. Of course, it is easy to mock at prophecies of this kind on the score of their encouragement of moral laxity and so forth, but morality does *not* consist in going back to Noah's Ark—

Light from the East

however much some folk may regard it in that light.

And as to *Communism*, when every tiny news-sheet of to-day is rejoicing to add a word to its *condemnation*, that fact need not cause us any sort or kind of disturbance. On the contrary, it really proves that the thing so abused and vilified is in the air and closely impending—else indeed what cause were there to disown it? A thing which began ages ago with the first dawn of human life on the Earth is not destined to extinction now, and I may as well conclude with the following words from the same book (*Pagan and Christian Creeds*) which I have cited already: " So we come back to that with which we began—to Fear bred by Ignorance. From this source has sprung the long list of follies, cruelties and sufferings which mark the record of the human race since the Dawn of History." And to the overcoming of this Fear we perforce must look for our future deliverance, and for the discovery—even in the midst of *this*

The Endeavour to Control Desire

world—of our True Home. We may indeed say that since these two nightmares (Fear and Ignorance) have been the fertile cause of all our troubles it only remains for us to sit up and rub our eyes, and convince ourselves that they and their spectral brood exist no more!

BIRTH CONTROL AND BISEXUALITY

Birth Control.

THE enormous importance of Birth Control has, even yet, hardly been recognised. Indeed one is surprised to think that it is only lately that the subject has been at all seriously tackled. In previous ages positive checks, in the form of War, Disease, Malnutrition, Malsanitation, and a dozen other pests, have raged and flourished. But to-day, with the promised removal of these and the simultaneous increase in the amenities and securities of Life, we have come face to face with the threat of an almost limitless increase of population, and it is certain that in the mass—not having realised the new conditions, we shall be quite unprepared to deal with that increase. At any

Birth Control and Bisexuality

moment now we may be confronted with famines, wars, raids, lootings, destruction of settled life and security, and a hundred other problems (arising from over-population) for whose solution we have no ready framed programme, and which will plunge us into dire confusion and anarchy.

In a former paper[1] I have pointed out how from the early ages of the world there has been some strange instinct impelling humanity almost to crucify itself in the endeavour to crush out the sex impulse and the instinct of race propagation—which in some form or other seems to underlie all organic life; but this monkish tendency, though excusable in certain cases, is quite unreasonable on the whole, and indeed, in a sense, quite futile; the desire will never be crushed out, though, as I have said before, it is quite likely that it will take on a form somewhat different from its present one.

Are we then to put off action until, with hardly standing room left, the denizens of

[1] *The Endeavour to Control Desire*

Light from the East

our planet turn upon each other like so many starving wolves in mutual and mad destruction, or are we to use what (little?) good sense we have left, and decide that the only reasonable course is to refuse (before it is too late) to bring into the world more children than we can actually provide for. No one can size up the problem so far without seeing that there is only one human and rational answer, namely birth control. Think of the condition of Japan. Count Michimasa Soyejima predicts war there from sheer pressure of the population [1] within the next ten years unless birth control becomes general before that time; or think of China, from which country a member of the University of Chicago writes: "I am completing my course here in February and returning to China. If there is any country in the world that *needs* to control birth, it is my country."

Plato, whose life more than 2,000 years ago was devoted to the discussion of what

[1] *Birth Control Review*, February 1926.

Birth Control and Bisexuality

institutions were best for an ideal community, concluded that *to limit the population to a fixed number was a first necessity,* because only under such a condition could men see clearly the outline of the problem with which they had to deal; and though under our modern conditions any idea of limiting population to that extent seems rather hopeless, we can perceive only too clearly the justice and the point of Plato's contention.

The propaganda of Birth Control has hitherto been chiefly supported and energised by *Women*—in which fact we see partly the superior sensitiveness of Women to the needs of the general community, and partly their (perfectly natural and sensible) sensitiveness to their *own needs*. Too long has social life suffered, and its advance been retarded under the rather stupid and blundering Man-made laws which have hitherto obtained, and too long have Women themselves been crippled under the same regime;

Light from the East

but now we see that a swing of the pendulum is taking place, and with it a quite natural revolt from the old conditions.

We have not uncommonly in public galleries admired some ancient bas-reliefs and sculptures, of wars between Greeks and Amazons—a Greek, for example, seizing an Amazon by the hair of her head and shamefully discomfiting her. "I didn't know," says an onlooker, "that the Greeks could ever have behaved in such an *ungentlemanly* way, treating women like *that*." But these sculptures (I need hardly say) did not emerge from modern drawing-rooms, but were transcripts of scenes witnessed in actual life; and belong to a period when "gentlemen" did not exist, and Men had undoubtedly to fight at times—even in self-defence—against the invasions of the Female Sex. There is a well-known play of Aristophanes in which, in order to punish the Men, the women are represented as banding themselves together to abstain from all sexual intercourse until such time as the men should

Birth Control and Bisexuality

come to heel and confess themselves beaten. They, the women, are represented as exhorting each other (notwithstanding all temptations to the contrary) to remain firm and faithful in their effort to subdue the men by a determined aloofness.

Probably this cleavage between the two sexes is of quite ancient origin. Plato, both in the *Republic* and in the *Laws*, held that the population must be kept stationary, and that on the average there should be two children (a boy and a girl) for each family. About the methods for effecting this he is not very precise (I am here quoting from a friend who is an accomplished classical scholar), but he, Plato, suggests that if there are more children in one family, the surplus should be distributed to families having no children or only one child. Also he suggests emigration as, in some cases, a possible remedy. In the *Republic* (since all children were to be brought up by "the Guardians" and not even to know who their parents were) all sex-intercourse was to

Light from the East

be regulated by the State and to be directed to the production of the best possible breed or breeds.

Aristotle, in his picture of the Ideal State, has the same views about the need of a stationary population. And as to contraceptives, the Greeks do not seem to have known about their use; but infanticide was certainly practised.

To return to the important point that the subject of Birth Control has been chiefly organised and engineered by women, this must not make us blind to certain defects in the way in which it has been handled. The tendency of men to seek variety in their love-affairs has sometimes been turned into a charge against them and into an accusation —an accusation of mere frivolity. But I regard that as most foolish and ill-judged. Men, no doubt, *need* variety, and without it they could hardly fulfil their real natures; Woman—one may say—is by nature sessile, and though many women cultivate a kind of superficial gaiety and sparkle, their very

Birth Control and Bisexuality

effort in that direction is often a weariness to themselves, and only too obvious to onlookers. Even Havelock Ellis, who is so wonderfully fair and balanced in his criticisms, quotes Michelet about *Antaeus* who (it will be remembered) was supposed only to regain his strength by actual contact with his Mother Earth. "Just in the same way" (says Ellis) "man regains his normal strength by contact with women, and when exhausted by the buffetings of life comes back again and again to her, to renew his vitality." This may indeed, in the great average, be true, but my own experience, I am sorry to say, is just the reverse. Instead of women renewing one's vitality, I find that they sap and deplete us—many of us—to an almost fatal extent! This may seem an unfair charge, but for evidence and corroboration, I must call as witness a woman, who has herself been a great supporter of the feminine cause and whose writings have been for years a perfect armoury of facts and arguments in woman's *favour*—

Light from the East

I mean that great and original authoress, Olive Schreiner. I knew Olive Schreiner fairly intimately, and at times saw a good deal of her, and like everyone else who knew her, had the *greatest respect* for her mental penetration and vigour; but her words on the parasitic nature and habits of women—I suppose from their close agreement with my own experience—have ever stuck in my mind. Such a parasitic nature and habit is (as Ellis and others have pointed out) perfectly natural and normal in the sex—or perhaps one ought to say *was*, for almost as one writes one can see that the situation is rapidly changing. Women having been brought up from countless years in the past in positions of dependence on, and subservience to, men, have developed by necessity an adaptation to such positions. Now, however, and fortunately, as I say the situation is rapidly changing. One can hardly express sufficiently one's admiration for the frank outspokenness of the modern girls and young women; and when I think of the conditions

Birth Control and Bisexuality

under which my own sisters, for instance, grew up, fifty years ago, I can hardly with sufficient warmth express my gratitude for the change which has taken place.

It might almost be reckoned as a law of Nature, that when, in the gradual expansion of activities which we call Evolution, this expansion or growth is at any point checked and confined, the expansive tendency will find its way out at some neighbouring point. Something of the kind does undoubtedly happen in the development of a plant or a tree; the bark strangulates growth for a time, and then the inner forces, gathering strength, push their way out in the form of an adjacent leaf or bud. So when (not without much suffering and tribulation) the young women of fifty years ago found themselves debarred from their natural outlet in family life and normal sexuality, a similar thing happened and the compensation came in the form of a great outgrowth of political activity (women's suffrage, etc.). It is possible that the period of sex-repression

Light from the East

through which our girls and young women have passed is going to justify itself in a coming period of considerable artistic expansion and development. I profoundly hope that it will. It is not perhaps clear why Birth Control, acting to repress the child-bearing functions, should be expected to have its compensation in a growth of *artistic* interest and capacity; but after all the most important *art-work* possible to humanity *is* the rearing of worthy children, and in that sense it does seem quite possible that Birth Control, by diminishing the *number* of children born into the world, may re-act in a great improvement in their *quality*. Again we profoundly hope that it will so re-act.

Bisexuality

It is generally agreed that in the case of either sex the *rudiments* of the organs of the opposite sex are to be found. This is a matter of actual physiology and fact. In any ordinary boy there are indication of

Birth Control and Bisexuality

the breasts of a girl. In many girls and young women the beginnings of a moustache can be traced. It would seem that in quite early stages of development the two Types, male and female, tend to occur combined and to overlap, and it is only at a later stage, and with maturity, that they diverge along their different paths. It may almost be said that the child is bisexual, it has both natures, masculine and feminine; and its affections, devoid of strictly sexual intent, are given to girls and boys alike.

However, there comes a time when Nature, or social life, or the growth and unfolding of elements hitherto hidden, compel the child to range itself definitely on one side or the other—*as* a boy or as a girl. It does not follow, of course, that *all* the elements—at this critical age—take the same direction; one child, though of girlish disposition in general, and even a girl in actual sexual conformation, may take very heartily to cricket or baseball; another child, of boyish habits and even dress, may love embroidery

Light from the East

and needlework; the variety of temperament and tendency is too great to be susceptible of reduction to any fixed schedule or system. We all know Women (in appearance) who —so we say—are "really Men"; or Men who are "half" Women. On the stage, naturally, these cross-tendencies exhibit themselves pretty freely; or perhaps one ought to say that those boys and girls who have these cross-tendencies already in them very naturally *select* the stage as their profession, and that the stage with its enormous variety of types provides plenty of material for such cases.

Again, it is hardly necessary to say—and certainly needless to labour the point—that in the matter of offspring, such cross-types are not, as a rule, very prolific. Men and women of the double nature do not have large families—and one can hardly expect that of them. The male of that type does not pursue the female *à outrance*. He is too diffident in his love-affairs and easily repulsed. The female of the same type

Birth Control and Bisexuality

does not, as a rule, rouse the male by pretended shyness and flight, but is more likely to quench his ardour by argument! These facts are very necessary to be known, not only by prospective parents, but also by judges and magistrates, who often through sheer ignorance make gross mistakes and whose sentences are in consequence not infrequently mere travesties of justice.

There are many indications that bisexuality and the evolution of a human type which will be *median* in character—i.e. neither excessively male nor excessively female—may be expected in the future. And if so, it seems not unlikely that the knotty question with which we began this chapter, that of birth-limitation, will resolve *itself* without recourse to any Platonic or Malthusian formulæ. The bisexual types, or those tending that way, will automatically result in the production of smaller families, and the burning question of Birth Control will cease to have the same practical significance in the future as it has had in the past.

Light from the East

In the little book on *The Psychology of the Poet Shelley* which my friend Guy Barnard and I published in 1925, the fringe of this great question is touched. Shelley was much in advance of his age, and he inevitably roused people's interest in many new problems. One of these (see *The Witch of Atlas*) was the possibility of a new type arising of human being, who should in a sense *combine* the qualities of the two sexes— a being having the grace of both sexes, and full of such dreams as would one day become the inspiration of a new world-order, yet of such a nature that its love would *not* be dependent (as indeed most loves now are) on mere *sexual* urge and corporeal desire, "but would be a vivid manifestation of the universal creative Life, in the body even as in the soul."[1] Large families, which owing to English marriage-customs of that period *were* very common, have now gone out of fashion. They were the result of what Plato calls the *pandemic love*, the kind

[1] See *The Psychology of the Poet Shelley*, p. 30.

Birth Control and Bisexuality

of love favoured by the mass-peoples, and sexual or sensual in its main outlines; but now the accepted type of love has to a certain extent changed. With the fusing or blending of the two temperaments—the masculine and the feminine—there has come about, perfectly naturally and without effort or violent reaction, a new type of devotion, more serene, more equable, more long-lasting—more perhaps resembling the type of devotion with which we are familiar as between two comrades of the same sex. There has come about a considerable development of interest in what may be called "Other-world problems"—life after death, divination, the attainment of higher powers, etc. Speaking of divination, the authors of *The Psychology of the Poet Shelley* say (p. 45): "It is easy to suppose that those pioneers of an earlier world, those Apollos, Buddhas, Dionysus, Osiris, etc. (who once probably were men), were somewhat bisexual in temperament, and that it was largely owing to that fact that they were endowed

Light from the East

with far-reaching powers and became leaders of mankind." No one will contest the right of Shelley to our reverence as one of the great leaders of mankind, and it is interesting to find in Mr. Barnard's section of the book on *The Psychology of Shelley*, from which I have just quoted, these words: "Shelley loved to create androgynous types. He loved the feminine qualities when they were in men, and the masculine qualities in women. It would seem as if he were continually striving to create an ideal *bisexual* character."

All this—and duly weighing Shelley's recognised place among the "leaders" of mankind—suggests that we are approaching a period when the Shelleyan ideals, and the meaning of the word "bisexuality" will be more generally recognised than they are to-day; and if so it seems to follow that that period will be one in which the present troubles arising from over-density of population will be passing—or will have passed—away.

THE MOUNA SWAMIS AND THE ANIMALS

WE have heard of Trappists and others who have vowed themselves to perpetual silence; and it seems quite credible that even ordinary folk may favour a practice of this kind, if only as a means of defence against the eternal stream of idle talk—in the street or in the market-place or the drawing-room. Someone has characterised the mania of incessant loquacity, which afflicts some people, as *a physical disease*—a " determination of words to the mouth "; and indeed the semi-medical complexion of the term may help one to realise that a nervous or constitutional defect may often underlie such cases—which should excite pity rather than blame—cases in which the

Light from the East

stream of talk can hardly be checked without resort to something like an operation !

There are among the Gñanis of India and Ceylon some who adopt a policy of Silence ; but it is obviously useless to ask them *why* they adopt it, because the question would remain up in the air and without reply ! The fact remains that there are some who keep to that practice, and who nevertheless are *highly reverenced*. They are called Mouna Swamis (Silent Masters). In the present chapter, however, I propose to speak not about these Gñanis, but about the Animals themselves—most of whom are entitled, I am sure, to be thus—and very respectfully—addressed.

The Animals, of course, have learned from Nature (and their own souls), and we likewise can learn from Nature and our own Instincts (if we respect the latter and keep them clean and healthy). For indeed the animals, while refraining from speech, show such extraordinary intelligence and sensitiveness that we are sometimes inclined to

The Mouna Swamis and the Animals

think that their speechlessness arises more from unwillingness than from inability. One of the most interesting books on this subject of the Animals that I have ever read is *Alone in the Wilderness*, by Joseph Knowles.[1] Mr. Knowles in 1913 went out into the woods of Maine, U.S.A., and lived there for two months leading a sort of Robinson Crusoe life: and that with absolutely *none* of the appliances of civilisation to assist him (in case he fell ill or suffered from cold or exposure, or met with any kind of accident) —without a gun, in fact, or a medicine bottle! And his venture, it must be said, was wonderfully happy and successful; some of his conclusions indeed are well worth recording and may interest my readers. Contrary to his own expectation the thing that proved the greatest trial to Joseph Knowles was not insufficiency of food or of clothing, but want of *society*. From the first he found that

[1] Published by Longmans, Green & Co. in 1914, but now (1926) out of print; though I hear that copies may possibly be obtained from Small, Maynard & Co., publishers, Boston (Mass.). U.S.A.

Light from the East

the effort to live alone and without human companionship was his chiefest cause of suffering. He realised how important, how *necessary*, to man is some kind of intercourse with his fellows, and how *cruel*, indeed how *wicked*, is much of our penal code which condemns criminals—often gentle and affectionate human beings—to *solitary confinement*—all the more cruel and wicked because in solitary confinement the instinct of helpfulness—one of the most precious and valuable of human virtues—is almost inevitably crushed out and killed. The unfortunate prisoner feels, and in many cases *knows*, that he is losing his divine prerogative and being thrust down to a lower level of humanity than that which rightfully belongs to him. The following quotations are from Mr. Knowles' above-mentioned book:

"While I always had an inherent love for wild animals my contact with them during my two months alone in the wilderness has made me love them even more. I was in truth one of them. They were my neighbours, my companions, my friends. Their proximity meant

The Mouna Swamis and the Animals

much to me, especially at the times when I was most depressed. I even talked with them, and, in their own way, they talked back to me. I felt confident that in six months' time every creature in that particular part of the wilderness would have known me and become friendly."

"There is a great deal to be learned from animals. Discontentment is unknown among them. They are individually free, go when and where they please, and do whatever they wish to do. Discontent in me had come as one of the results of a civilised life. . . . Men and Women of the world are nothing but animals called human beings—a polite name, that is all. Fundamentally they are no different from the animals that roam the woods. . . .

"Whenever I chanced to come across a deer on one of the trails, that deer knew instinctively the moment she saw me whether or not I had an idea of doing her harm. She understood me very quickly, and I understood her. That is why the red deer and the little white fawn that came to my spring every morning were such good friends of mine. There isn't an animal in the forest that doesn't *want* to make friends with man!"

"Since I have come back to civilisation hundreds of people, with real sympathy in their voices, have said to me, 'How you must have suffered!'

"In every instance they referred to physical suffering. They imagined themselves out in the dark woods, alone, and cold, and without any clothing. They thought of eating nothing but berries and roots, and with fertile imaginations, coloured by extreme contrasts between wilderness life and the life of civilisation, conjured up quite terrible pictures in their minds."

"They were all wrong. I did not experience any physical suffering to speak of, though I did suffer greatly in another way. My suffering was purely mental and a hundredfold worse than any physical suffering I experienced."

"Before I entered the forest I had never given a serious thought to the *mental* side of the question. I wanted to get away from the sham side of modern life, and from people; and I looked forward to being alone, where I could have a chance to think out various problems without interruption. It never occurred to me that I might be lonely."

"In past years I had often been in the woods alone, though, to be sure, not for very long at a time. In those days the solitude would be broken by the appearance of some chance hunter once in a while, and my talking with him would break the monotony until someone else came along. But here alone in the wilderness day after day without the sound of a human voice, or the contact of a human being, and the knowledge that there wouldn't be either for two whole months, it was very different."

"The complete isolation got on my nerves. It was far harder for me than it was for the original primitive man. *He* not only had his own kind about him, but he knew nothing of any other life than the one he was leading. *I* always had a comparison before me. *Before* I went

The Mouna Swamis and the Animals

into the woods the only thing which really puzzled me was whether or not I could stand the cold without clothes.[1] Afterwards this side of the question was a mere nothing compared with the mental torment, which I had completely overlooked." ...

"The torture always commenced with pictures of my friends and those I loved best coming into my mind. My heart was with them. I would dream of them as their faces rose before me in the firelight. When finally I dropped off into a troubled sleep I would keep right on seeing them in my dreams. Time and again those mental spells were almost too much for me. At those times I would vow that I would leave the forest on the very next day."

"I had a flock of partridges in the woods so tame that two of them would actually follow behind me on the trail. I used to laugh at them. They were jealous for fear one would get nearer to me than the other. Whenever one would come quite close to me the other would peck at him and drive him back. One morning I came across four or five of these birds on the lower limb of a tree. As I went closer and began talking to them they daintily sidestepped on that limb for all the world like a lot of coquettish young women. Finally it got so that I could put out

[1] Later on, Mr. Knowles found what might be expected, that clothing of some kind was *at times* quite necessary; and such as he needed he made for himself out of materials which the woods supplied.

Light from the East

my hand and touch them. They knew I wouldn't hurt them; but *under such conditions I never caught a partridge; it would have been a breach of confidence.*"[1] (P. 95.)

"As to the deer," the passage continues, "they will get so tame that they will come right up to your lean-to and eat out of your hand. You cannot tame deer by going to them. Arouse their curiosity, and show that you will not harm them. While they are still curious they will never forget you. They see and smell you, and their curiosity will bring them back. You don't have to go near any wild or domestic animal to tame it. It will come to you and live with you and sleep with you. All you have to do is simply to conceal your own curiosity."

"If an animal knows that you saw him and yet went about your own business without offering to harm him, that animal will never forget you. . . . It is not man that the wild animal is afraid of, but the human scent. This may have meant injury to some of his forbears and so he naturally inherits the instinctive fear. He (the animal) can instinctively read a man's character by his smell. And this is the reason why a deer will fly from one person the moment he gets his scent, while he

---

[1] Would that this italicized passage could be taken literally to *heart*. It is the deceit and betrayal with which we treat the animals which cause them to extend the same treatment to us. —E. C.

The page references are to the book, *Alone in the Wilderness*.

The Mouna Swamis and the Animals

will stand by and watch out of curiosity another man who means him no harm."[1] (P. 97.)

"Nature is the source from which we live and move and have our very being. Liberty is the foundation of good government. Yet nowhere does liberty exist so strongly as among the animals and in the heart of nature. From wilderness life to the simple country life, and then up through the life of a great city liberty gradually *decreases*.

> 'At gold's superior charm all freedom flies,
> The needy sell it and the rich man buys.'

The top-notch of society has the least liberty in the world, being bound hand and foot to a rigid social code." (P. 98.)

"Don't think for a moment that you can say to any ugly dog 'Nice doggy' in a voice that is quavering with fear, and get away with it ! The dog won't pay any attention to the 'nice doggy' part, but he will scent that fear." (P. 99.)

It will be seen from these quotations that the author of the book (Knowles)

[1] We may compare here the strange intuition of character which the *Gñanis* (like the animals though in a different way) seem to have. In my dealings with one or two of the Gñani class I was immediately conscious of the interpenetration (or contact) of the Gñanis mind with my own; and I think something of the same kind is true of our relation with the animals.—E. C.

Light from the East

has a keen insight into the characters of the various animals and into the justness of their response to human beings and human character. In one passage (page 129 of *Alone in the Wilderness*) he says:—

"There is no question in my mind as to whether or not animals have souls. Of course they have. If you have ever lived alone in the wilderness you will thoroughly believe that they have. Ask any man who has spent much of his time in the forest. Ask him about the squirrels he has watched, or the birds on certain trees that have sung and whistled to him. . . . They know who's who—these wood creatures—and can size up a man much better than a human being can size up one of his own kind. To them such a man is only another animal like themselves. It is not necessary for a man to *speak* to an animal in order to establish an understanding."

. . . "If I could only live about twice the time allotted to the human race, it would be the height of my ambition to go back to the woods where, in perfect harmony, I could come to understand more about all these living wild creatures. I am confident that a complete understanding would eventually arise between man and animal." (P. 130.)

What a joy it is to hear a man speak like that!—and one who knows the wild animals

The Mouna Swamis and the Animals

so well! How much, how much, Man might learn from them!—their directness and, so to speak, *outspokenness* (about their own personal needs, as hunger, sex, the need of excretion, the choice of associates, etc., etc.).

> "'Why is it,' says the ordinary sportsman, 'that when I haven't my gun with me I always have such good chances for shots?'
>
> "'The answer is simple,' says Mr. Knowles. 'These animals know when a man is in the woods to kill them. They can feel that he is there for that purpose. At those times they keep out of his way. . . . No animal in the woods would fear man if he left his killing instruments behind him. In fact they want to become friendly, and through curiosity will come to man. That is why the red deer and the white fawn would eat out of my hand and why partridges actually followed me and allowed me to touch them. I never want to see an animal harmed unless it is through absolute necessity. Even under these conditions there is a regret when I am forced to kill one.'"

I think the reader will now see why in this chapter I speak of *Mouna Swamis*. These animals are indeed our Silent Teachers and I feel sure that association with them on

Light from the East

equal terms will, when it comes to pass, bring about a great and much needed change in ourselves—a growth and expansion of our Humanity.

In conclusion, I may mention two or three points which are in the book, but which I had accidentally overlooked. For instance with regard to the ability of the human skin to resist cold.

The verdict of a doctor who examined Knowles at the conclusion was as follows :—

"Subjected to the action and the stimulus of the elements Mr. Knowles' skin has become a perfect skin. It serves him as an overcoat because it is so healthful that its pores close *at once* and shield him from draughts and sudden chills."

Further, Mr. Knowles says :—

"That trip of mine into the wilderness means that I was literally born again.[1] The day I came forth from the woods was the beginning of a new life for me. During my life in the world of civilisation I had never really given the time to think about things. I never really

[1] "Born again." More than once Mr. Knowles uses this expression to describe his experience.

The Mouna Swamis and the Animals

stopped to consider all the great advantages of Nature. . . . Those two months in the forest I sat time and time again in front of my camp fire and really thought for the first time in my life. It seemed as if every experience I ever had came back to me in the most minute detail. This made my brain worth something to me. In a word, my two months in the woods have been a wonderful education. The experience made me find myself.

"It showed me that there were thousands of things in our present so-called 'civilised' life that are unnecessary: in fact, foolish, ridiculous, wasteful—practices that stand in reality for nothing. It established for me the realisation that people are slaves to luxury, and that luxury is making great inroads on the mind and health. My friends know that the *notoriety*, which perhaps has come as a result of this experiment, means nothing to me."

With these last words about the notoriety which the experience brought to Mr. Knowles, one must cordially agree. How could that notoriety, to a man who had had such experiences, convey anything, except perhaps the desire to escape from it!

"According to my opinion the way the world is living at present is entirely wrong. Civilisation has carried us along to a point where, through custom and habit, we are accepting an artificial life rather than a natural one. Commercialism and the mad desire to make money have

Light from the East

blotted out everything else, and as a result we are not living, but merely existing.

"And just as I have said that children should live close to nature, so do I believe the same thing as applied to women. No man should expect a woman to slave at housework which would have the tendency to keep her constantly confined to the house. Nine-tenths of the nervous trouble among women to-day is caused by a lack of fresh air and exercise. . . . For two months I walked continually about the forest, and all the time I was doing this I was getting into splendid condition. I had no one to wait upon me. . . . When I wanted some berries I had to go and pick them. I couldn't ask anyone to 'pass me the berries.' I was absolutely dependent on myself, and this condition proved of tremendous benefit to me. . . . Civilisation needs to learn this lesson of self-dependence more than anything else. The people of to-day need to stop leaning on the other fellow for what they want. Within themselves, if they only knew it, is a power they do not dream of—*in a word, let humanity be born again.*"

On that note I will stop. There are many other excellent things in the book; but it is not necessary to delay over them. The general trend of Mr. Knowles' conclusions is clear enough.

His friendly relation to the various animals

The Mouna Swamis and the Animals comes out in the following paragraph (p. 110) :—

"Had I had an 'at home' there in the wilderness, invitations would have been forwarded to the moose, deer, beaver, wild-cat, otter, mink, squirrel, fox, rabbit, partridge, chipmunk, blue heron, loon, wild goose, wild duck and hoot owl—for they were all my neighbours and friends."

C. E.

THE END